The Bazaar Stall

by the same authors
COME, HEAR AND SEE
TEN LITTLE FINGERS

THE BAZAAR STALL

MONICA STUART AND GILL SOPER

with drawings by Juliet Renny

Faber and Faber   London · Boston

First published in 1978
by Faber and Faber Limited
3 Queen Square London WC1

ISBN 0 571 11280 3

© *Monica Stuart and Gill Soper*

Filmset and printed in Great Britain by BAS Printers Limited, Over Wallop, Hampshire

British Library Cataloguing in Publication Data

Stuart, Monica
  The bazaar stall.
  1. Handicraft
  I. Title
  II. Soper, Gill
  745.5   TT155
  ISBN 0-571-11280-3
  ISBN 0-571-11289-7 Pbk

CONTENTS

* Include articles which can be made by **children**

INTRODUCTION

One of the most popular and successful ways of raising funds is to sell handmade goods at bazaars, fêtes, fairs and sales of work. This book contains a wide selection of gifts, household articles, toys, novelties and decorations which have been designed specifically for this purpose although, of course, they need never reach the bazaar stall and can be made simply as attractive presents for family and friends. All the articles are easy to make and indeed many can be tackled by children of 7 to 8 years and upwards*. Older children could manage many more. We have restricted the materials used to those readily available or inexpensive to buy and have simplified designs, patterns and methods as much as possible to allow for mass production and minimum wastage.

It is wise to plan your sale well in advance. Before deciding what to make, consider who will be coming to the sale, what they will want to buy and how much they will be willing to pay. If you expect some of your shoppers to be children, make sure there are plenty of small, pocket-money items. Bear in mind that gardening aprons may go down very well on a Horticultural Society stall but not so well at your daughter's Brownie Bazaar. Allow time to collect suitable materials from relatives and friends as almost every household can yield some useful bits and pieces. Keep an eye open in shops, markets and jumble sales for remnants and oddments, and select your projects to fit the materials available.

* An asterisk indicates all articles which are simple enough for children to make.

THINGS YOU WILL NEED

Each project in the book includes a list of the tools and materials required for that particular job so that you can collect together everything you will need before you begin. The following have been omitted from the lists as they are frequently needed and should always be readily available.

Sewing equipment and threads
Scissors. An old pair for paper and card and a good pair for fabric and leather
Pencil, tailor's chalk and crayons to mark card, material and leather
Ruler
Tape measure
Basic woodworking tools
Pinking shears. Very useful to prevent fraying and to make decorative edges

FABRICS

Materials with small, dainty prints can be used most effectively to cover containers, writing folders, mirrors, note pads and doll's house furniture. They also make very attractive patchwork. Laura Ashley cotton fabric is particularly useful, so if there is a Laura Ashley shop in your area look out for remnants and patchwork packs.

As an alternative to buying felt, use remnants of non-fraying knit fabrics. There are many dress-weight synthetics that are particularly suitable as a substitute.

MASS PRODUCTION

Try to have all your tools and materials for the job ready before you begin and decide on the quantity you intend to make. Once you are sure of the method, work through one stage at a time on a production-line basis. If you are working with friends, it is usually much quicker to take one process each.

DISPLAYING THE GOODS

Give each stall an eye-catching sign to indicate the goods being sold. If you can anchor a bamboo pole to each end of the stall, suspend a notice painted on shelf paper between the tops of them. Alternatively, fix a cardboard flag poster to the top of a single pole or mount a notice on a wall or window behind the stall. Use cardboard boxes to make a display platform on the stall, and cover it with a bright cloth or crêpe paper, securely pinned or taped to the table. To display the goods to best advantage arrange a sample of each mass-produced item on a display board or shelves behind your stall so that they can be clearly seen with the prices marked beside them. This will help to minimize the handling of the goods arranged on the stall. Standardize prices as much as possible and make sure all articles are clearly marked, well before the doors open. When necessary, display the goods to show their function. A sample of the 'Hanging wall pockets' (page 50) could be hung up and filled with sewing notions or writing equipment. The finger puppets (page 18) could be displayed on life-sized cardboard hands.

PATTERN MAKING

Some of the patterns in the book are worked out on squared grids, each square representing either 2·5 cm (1 in) or 5 cm (2 in). Ready marked graph paper can be bought, or the lines drawn accurately 2·5 cm (1 in) or 5 cm (2 in) apart on plain paper. Transfer the design to your squared paper by marking each point at which the pattern line crosses a grid line. Then join these points. It is well worth making a cardboard template if it is to be used many times. Paste the full-scale pattern onto a piece of card and add all the necessary markings to your finished pattern. Thread a piece of string through the pattern pieces or store them in a polythene bag, clearly marked with the name of the article. To transfer your pattern to the material, hold the template firmly in place on the wrong side of the fabric and draw the outline with tailor's chalk or crayon.

WORKING WITH GLUES

The glues used in this book have been confined mainly to two types which are:

Copydex: This is a thick white adhesive which we have used mainly for sticking leather, material and felt. The instruction leaflet supplied with the tube or jar will give full details for its use. Remember that it is generally sufficient to apply copydex to one surface only, but when joining fine fabrics, apply it sparingly to each surface and leave to dry. Instant adhesion will then be obtained.

Uhu: This is a clear, quick-drying, all-purpose adhesive suitable for most handicraft work. For most materials, spread a thin layer of Uhu on both surfaces, leave to dry for a minute and then press together.

Where we have simply listed 'glue' as a requirement for the job, virtually any glue will do.

WORKING WITH LEATHER

Leather is very costly so buy inexpensive offcuts or ask around for old leather or suede garments. You may find them at jumble sales too. However shabby they appear, the reverse side is generally as good as new. The back of a leather coat usually has a suede-like surface, while the reverse of a suede garment often has a lovely leather finish. Most of these can provide a sound and effective material for a large variety of leather goods.

Dismantle the entire garment before you begin. You will notice that the skins vary in thickness. Use the larger and thicker pieces for the biggest items and the smaller and thinner pieces for small goods. Transfer patterns to leather by marking on the wrong side with a pencil. Use sharp scissors, taking long, even cuts to avoid jagged edges. Use copydex with care, especially on suede surfaces. Allow surplus glue to dry before trying to remove it.

Lightweight leather can be seamed, right sides together, in the normal way, while heavier leather seams are best glued and topstitched, wrong sides together. Bearing in mind that you may wish to use the reverse of the original garment as the right side of the new item, we use the word 'right' to describe your chosen finished right side. We also refer to 'leather' throughout, though you may be using suede.

If you are sewing with a machine, use a heavy duty needle and a fairly long stitch. Remember to decrease the sewing foot pressure to accommodate the leather thickness. If sewing very thick leather by hand, it is a great help to run each piece of leather separately through the unthreaded machine to make holes for easier hand stitching; but make sure the holes correspond exactly. Otherwise you may need to buy a special leather sewing needle. This has a triangular point.

We include a few sample objects, to give you some ideas. The containers have simple zip or velcro fastenings and can be adapted to make purses, bags, pencil cases, tobacco pouches, comb cases, etc., of any size. Some leather is suitable for cutting into thin strips to make thonging for bead necklaces. Pieces of contrasting suede or leather can be sewn together to make patchwork shoulder bags, pencil cases and so on.

TOYS

Balloons

Balloons
String
Thick marking pens
Crêpe paper
Copydex

Blown-up balloons can give attraction and a small profit to your
stall, but if you have time, use some bright marking pens and
scraps of crêpe paper to add funny faces, tails, hair, etc.

Bean Bags

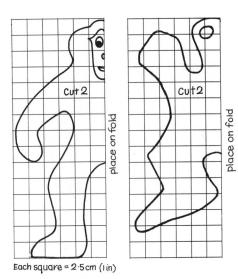

Each square = 2·5 cm (1 in)

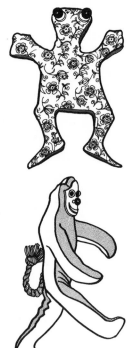

Material
Buttons or beads or 'eyes'
Felt for monkey face and lips and frog eyes
Cord, 15 cm (6 in), for monkey tail
Millet seed, approx. 1 lb for each bean bag

Place two pieces of material, right sides together, fold and cut out pattern. Make face on front before sewing front to back using small machine stitch and leaving 5 cm (2 in) gap at side. A 14-mm ($\frac{1}{2}$ in) seam allowance is given. Repeat stitching. Reinforce tight curves a third time. Trim away half of the seam allowance and clip tight curves. Turn and press. Fill with millet using funnel. Sew up gap. Sew on cord monkey tail securely.

12

Blackboard and Chalk

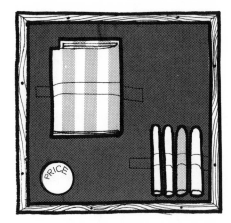

Plywood, 7 mm × 20 cm × 25 cm ($\frac{1}{4}$ × 8 × 10 in)
$\frac{1}{2}$ round dowel, 1 metre (1 yard)
Cloth
Chalk
Blackboard paint

Apply two coats of blackboard paint to board. Mitre the $\frac{1}{2}$ round dowel and nail around edge of board. For simplicity, coloured adhesive tape can be used instead. Fix cloth and chalks to board with transparent sticky tape. Cover set with transparent cling wrap.

Quick tip: The board can be adapted to hang in the kitchen as a shopping reminder.

Children's Note-Paper

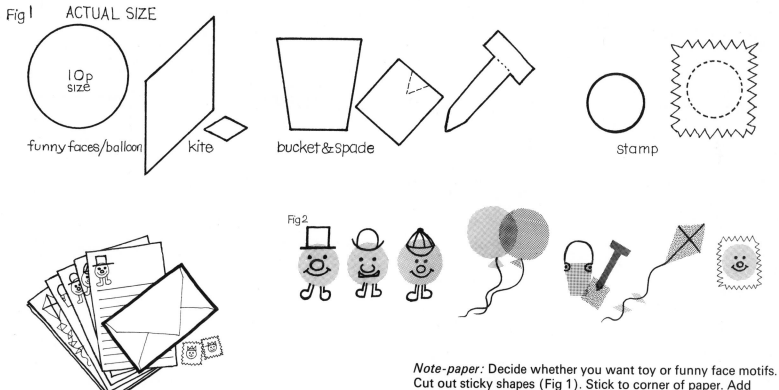

Fig 1 ACTUAL SIZE

10p size

funny faces/balloon   kite   bucket & spade   stamp

Fig 2

* This is suitable for **children** to make

Paper, approx 13 × 18 cm (5 × 7 in), coloured if obtainable
Envelopes
Coloured sticky paper
Black felt pen

Note-paper: Decide whether you want toy or funny face motifs. Cut out sticky shapes (Fig 1). Stick to corner of paper. Add details (Fig 2) and ruled lines with felt pen.

Stamps: Cut squares of sticky paper with pinking shears. Add funny faces (Figs 1 and 2). Pack in transparent cling film wrap.
  Put paper, envelopes and stamps in a paper or polythene bag. This can be sealed with a 'funny face' or stamp.

Quick tip: Bought sticky shapes can be used for the diamond kite shape and small round funny faces for stamps. If you have difficulty finding suitable paper, use typing paper cut to size.

Craft Sets

* These can be assembled by **children**. Pack them on polystyrene trays or cardboard covered with transparent cling wrap.

A CROCHET SET

Large crochet hook
Small balls of brightly coloured wool
Crochet instruction leaflet (optional)

C SEWING SET

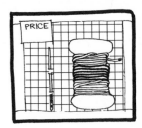

Binca material, approx. 30 × 30 cm (12 × 12 in)
Tapestry needle
Soft embroidery threads or tapestry wools wound onto a card

B KNITTING SET

Knitting needles
Small balls of brightly coloured wool
Knitting instruction leaflet (optional)

Doll's Cot or Pram Set

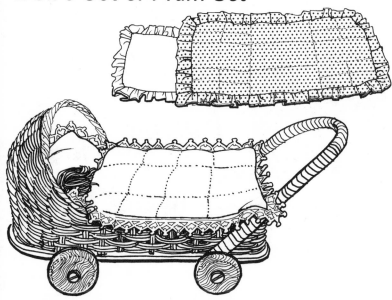

Pillow material, 2 pieces 20 × 25 cm (8 × 10 in)
Cover material, 2 pieces 33 × 40 cm (13 × 16 in)
Foam rubber or wadding, 1 piece 18 × 23 cm (7 × 9 in)
                     1 piece 30 × 38 cm (12 × 15 in)
Lace for edging, approx. 4 metres (4 yds)
Use 1½ metres (1½ yds) lace, gathered for pillow and 2½ metres (2½ yds) for cover.

With right sides together, stitch around 3 sides, sandwiching lace frill between the two layers. Stitch frill to fourth side of top layer. Turn to right side. Insert foam or wadding layer. Stitch final seam.
   The cover can be 'quilted' with lines of machine stitching.

Quick tip: Nylon quilted material can be used and an old housecoat may yield suitable pieces. A material frill can be made instead of using lace.

Doll's Food and Dishes

Nylon reinforced clay (no firing required)
Paints (most paints will do—see clay instruction leaflet)

Model an assortment of little pots, pans, dishes, loaves, pies, etc. Use a cocktail stick to make decorative markings. Paint in bright colours (we use model paints) and glue lightly to a piece of card before covering with transparent cling wrap.

Doll's House Furniture

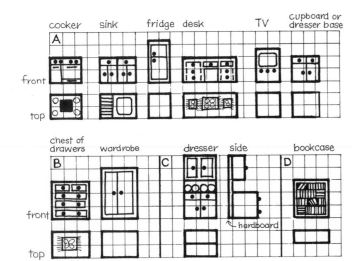

cooker   sink   fridge desk   TV   cupboard or dresser base

A

front

top

chest of drawers wardrobe   dresser side   bookcase

B   C   D

front

← hardboard

top

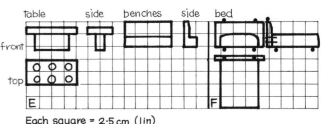

table   side benches side   bed

front

top

E   F

Each square = 2·5 cm (1 in)

A WOODEN BLOCK FURNITURE

Soft wood (planed)

A   Cut from 5 × 5 cm (2 × 2 in) wood
B   Cut from 5 × 8 cm (2 × 3 in)
C   Cut from 2·5 × 5 cm (1 × 2 in) and 5 × 5 cm (2 × 2 in)
D   Cut from 2·5 × 8 cm (1 × 3 in)
E   Cut from 1·5 × 5 cm (½ × 2 in) and 2·5 × 5 cm (1 × 2 in)
F   Cut from 2·5 × 8 cm (1 × 3 in) and 1·5 × 5 cm (½ × 2 in)

Round map pins
Self-adhesive freezer labels
TV picture
Lace braid
Fine black felt pen or china pencil
Coloured pencils
Material for bedding
Wood glue and copydex
Varnish

Saw and sand pieces of wood. The patterns give the basic sizes but bear in mind that the pieces will be slightly smaller as the wood will be planed. Mark lines with a fine felt pen. Colour books etc. with coloured pencils. Add freezer label sink, hotplates, plates etc. and glue picture to TV. Varnish all pieces (including labels). Add pin knobs. Glue on lace mats. Glue material over base of bed. Make bedspread, and pillow stuffed with cotton wool. Glue or stitch the material and lace.

B UPHOLSTERED FURNITURE

Soft wood, 1·5 × 5 cm (½ × 2 in) planed
Stiff cardboard
Foam sheet, 5 mm (¼ in) thick
Material (small print)
Cotton wool
Copydex

Sofa: Cut two 8 cm (3 in) lengths of wood. Glue the back to the seat and glue a layer of foam around this (Fig 1). Cover with material, gluing envelope seams at each end and overlapping edges underneath seat (Fig 2). For arms, cut out 2 pieces of stiff card, 4 cm high × 5 cm wide (1½ × 2 in). Cover with foam sheet (Fig 3) and material, gluing envelope seams at front and back with edges overlapping at seat line (Fig 4). Glue arms to seat. Sew the seams if you prefer.

Chair: Cut two 5 cm (2 in) lengths of wood and assemble as for sofa. The arms are the same as for the sofa.

Cushions: Small pieces of material stuffed with cotton wool. Sew or glue seams.

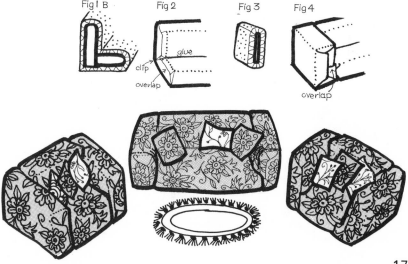

Fig1 B   Fig 2   Fig 3   Fig 4

Finger Puppets

Fig I
6·5 cm (2½ in)

body

A   FINGER PUPPET FAMILY

Ping-pong balls
Pink emulsion paint (or tint white paint with red powder or
   poster paint)
Felt
Lace, sequins, etc.
Waterproof felt pens
Glue

Using small pointed scissors, cut a hole, 12 mm (½ in) diameter,
in ball. Place on pencil and prop in plasticine or earth. Paint
pink. Glue edge of felt and form into cone (Fig 1). Glue tip and
insert into ball. Glue on felt hair (Fig 2), matching* with point
on ball opposite hole. Mark features with felt pens. Finish
figures with felt, lace, etc.

B   FINGER PUPPET ANIMALS

These are made in the same way as finger puppet people. Paint
balls appropriate colours. Add felt ears, cord tails, etc. Children's
books will provide ideas for animal faces.

Quick tip: Buy cheap ping-pong balls from toy shops.

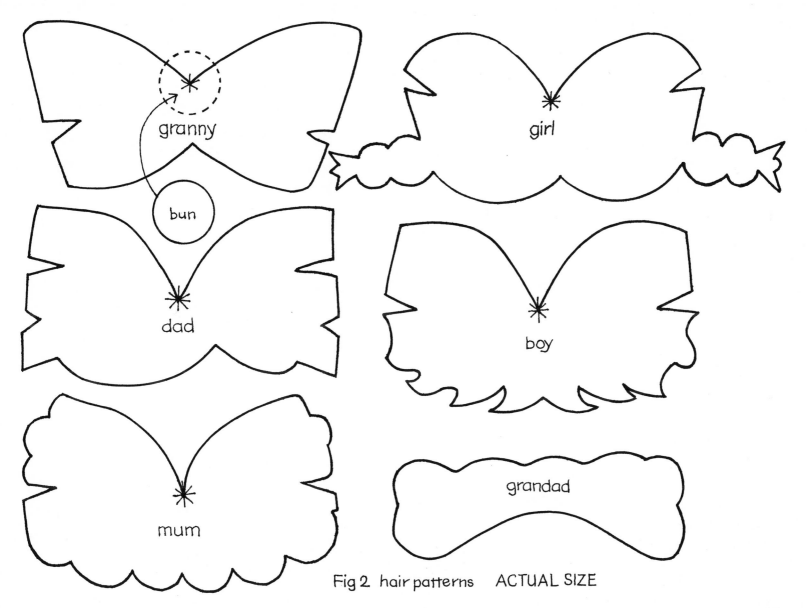

granny

bun

girl

dad

boy

mum

grandad

Fig 2 hair patterns   ACTUAL SIZE

19

Finger Puppet Theatre

Large cornflakes box
Wallpaper (small print)
Material, 25 × 40 cm (10 × 16 in)
Coathanger wire, 38 cm (15 in)
3 brass paper clips
Glue

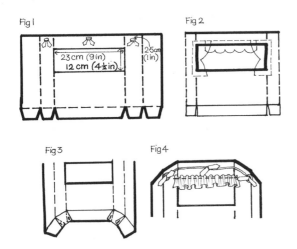

Remove top flaps of box, cut down centre back and open out flat. Cut out window and pierce top margin with paper clips (Fig 1). Lay flattened box on back of wallpaper and mark shape allowing 2 cm (½ in) overlap all round. Glue paper to box, covering paper clip heads. Cut out window and glue edges in the same way. Glue a strip of scalloped paper to top and side of window (Fig 2). Glue or staple base of box (Fig 3).

Curtains: Cut out valance and curtains. Use zig-zag machine stitch to save time when hemming edges. Gather valance and glue across top of window (Fig 4). Thread wire through top hem of curtain. Bend to fit top of window and fix with paper clips. Fig 4 shows wire with curtains omitted for clarity.
Quick tip: Glue hems and turnings with copydex instead of stitching.

Hand Puppets

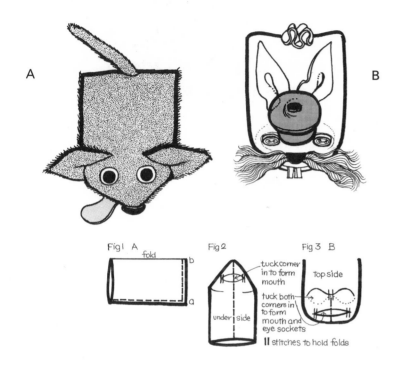

A

B

Fig 1 A
fold
b
a

Fig 2
tuck corner in to form mouth
tuck both corners in to form mouth and eye sockets
under side

Fig 3 B
Top side
II stitches to hold folds

* These can be made by **children**

Material, 23 × 23 cm (9 × 9 in) plus scraps for ears, etc. (See *Quick tips*)
Buttons, beads and felt for eyes, nose etc.
Copydex

A The dog is made of fur fabric. Stitch side and end of folded material (Fig 1). Turn glove to right side. Tuck in corner 'a' to form mouth (Fig 2). Sew on button eyes and felt nose and tongue. Cut out triangular ears and stitch to head, making a tuck at the base as you do so. The tail is a roll of fabric stitched in place.

B Make the rabbit in the same way but fold in corner 'b' also (Fig 3). The cap is a gathered circle of felt. Glue peak and band to cap and glue cap to head. Glue or stitch long, tucked ears to cap and head. Glue or stitch whiskers (frayed cord), nose and teeth in place. Sew on button eyes and a gathered circle of fabric for tail.

Quick tips: Use any sturdy, non-fraying material. Fur fabric, bonded material or felt are particularly suitable. Devise all sorts of animals—real or imaginary.

Hobby Horse

Firm material
Felt—white, blue (or make button eyes)
White cotton fringing, 36 cm (14 in)
Piping cord, 1 metre (1 yd)
Ribbon, 2·5 cm × 1 metre (1 in × 1 yd)
2 curtain rings
Stuffing (old stockings will do)
Foam rubber, small piece
Wood 2·5 cm × 2·5 cm × 1 metre (1 × 1 × 40 in) or use
　broom handle
Wood dowel, 1 cm ($\frac{3}{8}$ in) thick, 25 cm (10 in) long
Nails, 14 mm ($\frac{1}{2}$ in)
Wood glue
Copydex

Cut out head and ears (Fig 1), remembering to reverse head
pattern for the second piece if necessary. Stitch rings and glue
and stitch felt eyes in place (Fig 1). With right sides facing, and
sandwiching the fringing in between, sew the heads together.
Hem the neck edge. Stitch ears. Turn head and ears to right
side. Turn in and stitch bases of ears. Drill hole 38 cm (15 in)
from top of well-sanded stick. Glue and nail dowel in place.
Alternatively, glue and screw a simple cross bar to the stick. Fix
a piece of foam (or other padding) over the top of the stick with
a nail. Insert into head and stuff firmly. Do this out-of-doors if
using foam chips. Secure material at neck with a strong rubber
band and 4 nails. Add ribbon bow, fixing in place with glue or
stitching. Stitch ears in place, making a small tuck in base of
ears. Wind cord around nose and back through rings, tying
ends at neck.

Quick tip: For a special gift, a wheel can be fixed to the
bottom of the stick. These are obtainable from
hardware and D.I.Y. shops.

22

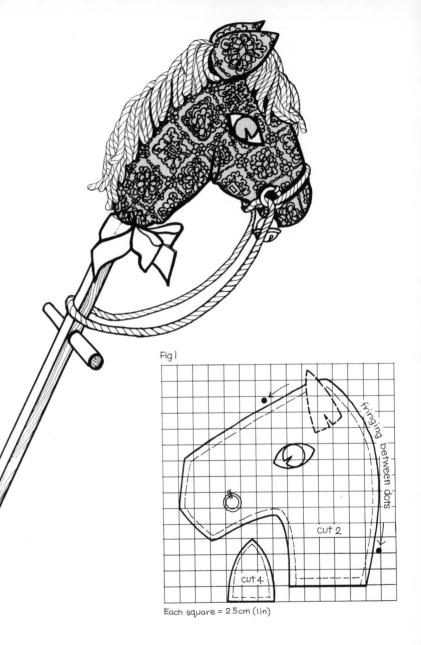

Fig I

fringing between dots

cut 2

cut 4

Each square = 2.5cm (1in)

Money Box

* This can be made by **children**

Large sweetie tube (collect these at Christmas)
Red paper, such as gift wrap or poster paper
White sticky label
Black felt pen
Glue or paste

Using sharp, pointed scissors, cut a slit, 14 mm × 4 cm ($\frac{1}{2}$ in × 1$\frac{1}{2}$ in), near the open end of the tube. Cut paper to fit and glue around tube. Snip paper at slit and glue edges inside tube. Glue paper to top and bottom. Add label marked with 'Collections' etc.

Quick tip: A large sticky paper square will fit around a 20 cm (8 in) tube.

Noughts and Crosses

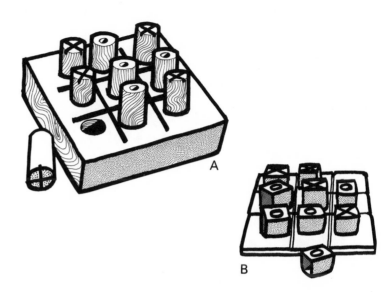

A Piece of wood for base, at least 14 mm ($\frac{1}{2}$ in) thick
   Wood dowel, 14 mm ($\frac{1}{2}$ in) thick, 23 cm (9 in) long
   Wood burner (optional)
   Varnish

Cut dowel into 9 pieces. Drill 9 corresponding holes, 14 mm ($\frac{1}{2}$ in) deep into wood. Use drill to mark O's on one end of peg and use saw to mark X's on the other end. Use wood burner to emphasize markings. Varnish set.

B *This can be made by **children**

   Nylon reinforced clay (no firing required)
   Paint (most paints will do: See clay instruction leaflet)

Make a simple slab base and cubes marked with O on one side and X on the opposite side. Paint. Cover set with transparent cling wrap.

Man of Action Equipment

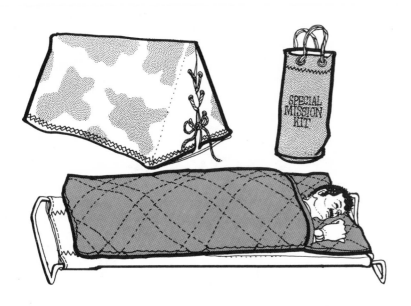

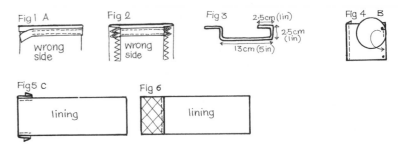

Fig 1 A — wrong side

Fig 2 — wrong side

Fig 3 — 2·5cm (1in), 2·5cm (1in), 13cm (5in)

Fig 4 B

Fig 5 C — lining

Fig 6 — lining

A CAMP BED

Material (sheeting will do), 17 × 33 cm (6½ × 13 in)
Tape, 2 pieces 2·5 × 17 cm (1 × 6½ in)
Wood dowel, 2 pieces 7 mm (¼ in) thick, 30 cm (12 in) long
Wire coathanger

Turn 1·5 cm (½ in) hem at each end of material and stitch tape on (Fig 1). Make 2 cm (¾ in) hems at each side, reinforcing stitching at each end (Fig 2). Slot a piece of dowel into each hem. To make legs, cut two 23 cm (9 in) lengths of wire. File the ends. Bend as shown in Fig 3. To do this, anchor the wire in a vice if you have one. Insert the wire ends into the hems, stretching the material taut.

B KIT BAG

Firm material, 20 × 20 cm (8 × 8 in) and an 8 cm (3 in) circle
String, 25 cm (10 in)
4 or 5 eyelets
Black felt pen

Allow 1·5 cm (½ in) for hem and seams. Hem top of bag. With right sides together stitch circle base to square. Start as in Fig 4 and ease circle around to match up seams between dots as you stitch. With right sides together, sew side seam. Turn bag to right side. Space eyelets around top of bag. Thread string through and tie ends together. Write 'Special Mission Kit' on bag.

C SLEEPING BAG

Material (quilted if possible—e.g. an old anorak)
Lining (sheeting will do)

Cut out material, both material and lining in the following sizes: 15 × 38 cm (6 × 15 in) and 15 × 28 cm (6 × 11 in). Place lining on wrong side of corresponding material and treat as one piece. Stitch 1·5 cm (½ in) hem at top end of each piece. Turn back top 5 cm (2 in) of long piece and stitch edges (Fig 5). Turn to right side and stitch hemmed edge (Fig 6). Place 2 pieces right sides together. Stitch seams. Turn to right side. Press if necessary.

D TENT

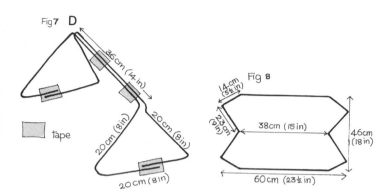

Fig 7 D

36 cm (14 in)

20 cm (8 in)
20 cm (8 in)
20 cm (8 in)

tape

Fig 8

14 cm (5½ in)
23 cm (9 in)
38 cm (15 in)
46 cm (18 in)
60 cm (23½ in)

2 wire coathangers
Self-adhesive tape, e.g. PVC insulating tape
Material (sheeting will do)
Paint (camouflage colours)—optional
String, or two 18 cm (7 in) zips

Straighten both coathangers. Anchor the wire in a bench vice if
you have one, or use pliers to bend as shown in Fig 7. Fix the 2
pieces together with sticky tape. Cut out tent (Fig 8). Make
1·5 cm (½ in) hem around raw edges. Make holes in edges of
flaps and lace with string (or sew zips in place). One end can be
sewn up if you prefer. Paint the tent with patches of camouflage
colour.

Marbles

Nylon reinforced clay (or bought marbles)
Paints (most paints will do: See clay instruction leaflet)
Plastic net bags
Cord or string

Roll clay into marbles. Paint. Pack in small, plastic nets, or make
drawstring bags out of fabric. Tie bags securely—loose marbles
can create problems.

Nurse's Outfit

To fit 3 to 6-year-old child

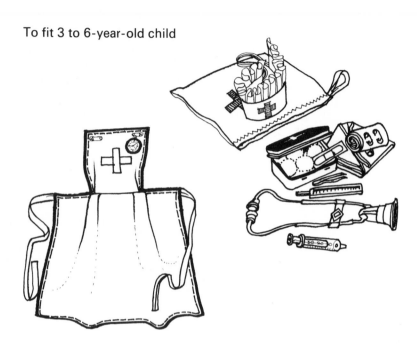

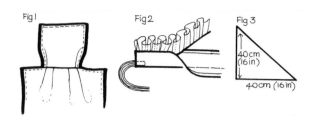

Fig 1   Fig 2   Fig 3

40 cm (16 in)

40 cm (16 in)

APRON

White material, 1 piece 30 × 50 cm (12 × 20 in)
1 piece 18 × 20 cm (7 × 8 in)
White tape, 2 pieces 35 cm (14 in)
Red tape or ribbon
2 safety pins
Plastic watch (optional)

Stitch hem around apron skirt and bib. Stitch bib to skirt making tucks in both (Fig 1). Add tapes to skirt and red cross and safety pins to bib.

HEADBAND

White material, 8 × 30 cm (3 × 12 in)
Lace, 2·5 × 45 cm (1 × 18 in)
Red tape or ribbon
Elastic, 20 cm (8 in)

Fold material in half lengthways, turning in narrow seam allowances. Stitch around edge of band, incorporating gathered lace and elastic (Fig 2). Add red cross.

DRAWSTRING BAG

White material, 25 × 45 cm (10 × 18 in)
Tape, 60 cm (24 in)
Red tape or ribbon

Fold material in half and stitch bottom and side seams. Make 14 mm (½ in) hem at top for drawstring. Add red cross.

KIT FOR NURSE'S BAG

Here are a few ideas:
Triangular bandage (Fig 3)
Small tin, marked with red cross and containing pins, bandage, sticky plaster and cottonwool
Toy stethoscope, syringe etc. from doctor's or nurse's set available at toy shops.

Painting Apron

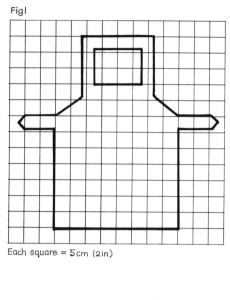

Fig1

Each square = 5cm (2in)

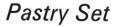

Fig2

━ PVC tape

Pastry Set

Heavy gauge polythene (See *Quick tips*)
Contrasting PVC tape
Sticky seals or motifs cut from fablon (optional)

Cut out apron (Fig 1) and 2 strips, 4 × 60 cm (1½ × 24 in). Stick strips of PVC tape along edge of neck and bib to reinforce and decorate apron (Fig 2). Tie on strips (unless polythene sheet is large enough to cut all in one). Make a word or motif from PVC tape or add a sticky seal or fablon motif.

Quick tips: Large freezer batching bags are obtainable in a variety of bright colours. Green rubbish bags are also suitable and clear, heavy duty polythene (often obtained with new furniture) can be brightened with colourful PVC tape.
  When cutting polythene, make long, even cuts to avoid jagged edges and tearing.

Hardboard, 18 × 25 cm (7 × 10 in)
Thick dowel, 18 cm (7 in) (See *Quick tips*.)
Small plastic pastry cutter (See *Quick tips*.)
Plastic knife
Cake cases

Fix the rolling pin, cutter and knife to board with transparent sticky tape. Cover with transparent cling wrap.

Quick tips: Cut up a broom handle to make rolling pins. We found a packet of 6 plastic novelty cutters in a toy shop, though ordinary round, fluted cutters will do.

Peg Dolls and Peg Doll Kit

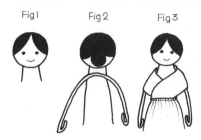

PEG DOLLS

'Dolly' pegs can be dressed in many different ways. Here is one very simple version. To save time, use glue instead of needle and thread except to gather skirt. Our pegs are 11 cm (4½ in). If yours differ from this, adjust the skirt length accordingly.

'Dolly' peg
Pipe cleaner, 8 cm (3 in)
Cotton material, 10 × 20 cm (4 × 8 in) for skirt
Wide lace or lacy material for apron
Scraps of lace, ribbon etc.
Fine black felt pen
Copydex

Mark face and hair (Fig 1). Glue pipe cleaner to peg (Fig 2). Glue skirt seam and gather to fit peg. Anchor at 'waist' with glue. Glue tucks in apron and glue to top of skirt. Glue piece of ribbon or lace over shoulders to form bodice (Fig 3). Glue band around waist to cover raw edges. Trim skirt with lace and glue a lace motif to head.

PEG DOLL KIT

Prepare a peg by marking face and hair and gluing on pipe cleaner arms. Pack with skirt material and lace etc. on a piece of card covered with transparent cling wrap.

Pencil Cases

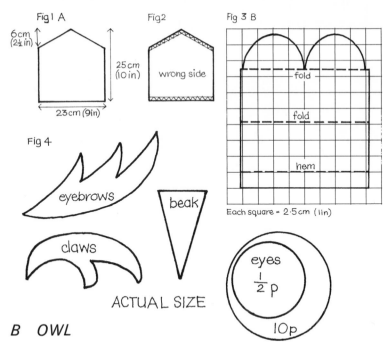

Fig 1 A

6cm (2½ in)

25cm (10 in)

23cm (9in)

Fig 2

wrong side

Fig 3 B

fold

fold

hem

Each square = 2·5 cm (1in)

Fig 4

eyebrows

claws

ACTUAL SIZE

beak

eyes ½ p

10p

A AIRMAIL ENVELOPE

Blue denim material, 23 × 25 cm (9 × 10 in)
Narrow ric-rac, red, ½ metre (¾ yd)
          royal blue, ½ metre (¾ yd)
Velcro fastening, 5 cm (2 in)
Iron-on tape
Air mail sticker
Used stamps
Copydex

Cut out denim envelope (Fig 1). Turn and topstitch 1·5 cm (½ in) hems using machine zigzag (Fig 2). Stitch velcro on right side close to straight hem edge. With right sides together, stitch side seams. Glue red ric-rac around border, close to edge. Glue blue ric-rac to border, overlapping red slightly and matching zigzags. You may need to snip it at the corners. Iron name tape in place, for owner to add his own name and address. Glue air mail sticker and stamps in place, making sure all edges and corners are secure. Stitch remaining velcro to reverse side of flap.

Quick tip: The reverse side of an old denim garment may be suitable for this.

B OWL

Leather
Velcro fastening, 4 cm (1½ in)
Copydex

Cut out leather (Fig 3). Turn lower edge to wrong side to make 2·5 cm (1 in) hem. Glue down. With right sides together, stitch 7 mm (¼ in) side seams. Turn to right side. Trace and cut out eyebrows and claws, reversing pattern for second of each pair. Cut out beak and eyes (Fig 4). Use the wrong side of the leather for contrast (except eye pupils). Place these features onto owl and mark position of eyes. Cut velcro in half and glue and stitch in place so that stitching will be covered by eyes. Glue features in place.

Quick tips: You can use large snap fasteners instead of velcro. Glue circles of leather over stitching behind lower pair to reinforce. See 'Working with leather' (page 9).

29

Purses

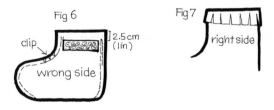

Fig 6
clip
2.5 cm (1 in)
wrong side

Fig 7
right side

Fig 1 A
cut 2

Fig 2
right side

Fig 3
2.5 cm (1 in)
wrong side

Fig 4
ACTUAL SIZE

Fig 5 B

Each square = 2·5 cm (1 in)

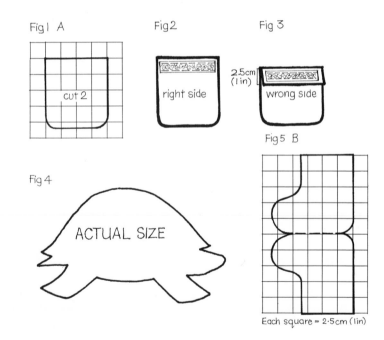

A   LEATHER PURSE

Leather
Velcro fastening, 8 cm (3 in)
Copydex

Cut out purse (Fig 1). Glue and stitch velcro to the top of each piece of leather, on the right side (Fig 2). Fold this to wrong side and glue down (Fig 3). Glue seams, wrong sides together. When dry, topstitch around seam.
Cut out a tortoise (or other shape) from contrasting leather (Fig 4). Glue to purse.

B   LEATHER BOOT PURSE

Leather
Velcro fastening, 8 cm (3 in)
Copydex

Cut out boot shape (Fig 5). Glue and stitch velcro to wrong side (Fig 6). With right sides together glue and stitch 7 mm ($\frac{1}{4}$ in) side seams (Fig 6). Turn boot to right side. Snip a fringe along top of boot and glue down to right side (Fig 7). Glue 7 mm ($\frac{1}{4}$ in) strips of leather (use wrong side for contrast) to boot to represent the lace with a bow at the top.

Quick tips: If the velcro is glued in place with care, following the copydex instructions, then stitching should not be necessary. However, it does give added reinforcement. See 'Working with leather' (page 9).

C FELT PURSE

* This can be made by **children**

Felt, 1 piece 10 × 18 cm (4 × 7 in)
     1 piece 2 × 8 cm ($\frac{3}{4}$ × 3 in)
     Scraps for motif
Curtain ring
Copydex
Pinking shears

Two purses can be made from one 23 cm (9 in) felt square. Cut out felt pieces. Fold the larger piece in half and shape lower corners. Fold the smaller piece over the ring and glue 2 sides together. Topstitch around bottom and side, incorporating the ring tag. Glue on a felt motif.

Quick tips: Children may find the stitching easier if the edges are glued together first. Pinking shears can be used to give a decorative edge.

Stamps

* These can be assembled by **children**

Used stamps
Stamp hinges

Ask children to save their 'swaps' and stick a selection to a postcard using stamp hinges. Cover card with cellophane or transparent cling wrap.

Pencil Tops

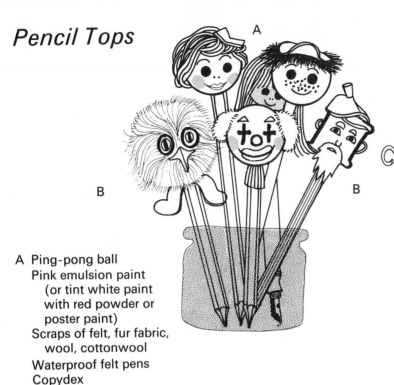

A Ping-pong ball
  Pink emulsion paint
    (or tint white paint
    with red powder or
    poster paint)
  Scraps of felt, fur fabric,
    wool, cottonwool
  Waterproof felt pens
  Copydex

Make hole in ping-pong ball with sharp, pointed scissors, so that ball fits snugly over pencil. Paint ball. Mark face. Glue on hair (wool, cottonwool or fur). Add felt hat, bow, etc.

Quick tips: Buy cheap ping-pong balls from toy shops. See page 18 for more ideas.

B Cotton reel
  Scraps of fur fabric, felt
  Copydex

Cover reel with felt or fur fabric. Add felt features. If the reel fits rather loosely over pencil, wedge a blob of plasticine in the hole.

Quick tip: *Children will find 'furry monsters' quite simple to make.

Pull-Along Barge

Wood, 2·5 × 5 × 33 cm (1 × 2 × 13 in) for barges
        2·5 × 2·5 × 15 cm (1 × 1 × 6 in) for cargo
Wood dowel, 1 cm ($\frac{3}{8}$ in) thick, 15 cm (6 in) long for cargo and funnel
3 small screw hooks and eyes
Bright paint (if using thick powder or poster paint, finish with varnish)
String
Wood glue

The pointed barge is 13 cm (5 in) long with a 5 cm (2 in) funnel glued into a drilled hole. The other two are 10 cm (4 in) long. Cut the remaining wood into 2·5 cm (1 in) crates and barrels. Paint all pieces. The crates can be marked with china pencil or felt pen. Add hooks, eyes and string. Pack the cargo in transparent cling wrap and all pieces in a polythene bag.

Sunflower Measure Poster

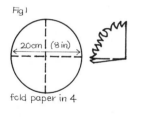

Fig 1
20cm (8 in)
fold paper in 4

Fig 2

Wall lining paper, 28 × 1 m 68 cm (11 × 66 in)
Stiff card, 2 pieces 4 × 27 cm (1½ × 10½ in)
Black felt pen
Thick green marking pen
Green paint
Yellow felt, 20 cm (8 in) circle
Brown felt, 11 cm (4½ in) circle
Glue

Fold back 5 cm (2 in) of paper at top and bottom of poster. Glue down, sandwiching a piece of card to stiffen. Sketch sunflower stem and leaves with pencil. Mark outlines with thick green marking pen. Paint over design with a green wash. Cut out paper sunflower pattern (Fig 1). Use this to make yellow felt flower head. Cut out brown felt flower centre with pinking shears. Glue flower to poster. Using a yardstick if you have one, mark measurements with black felt pen. Mark feet and inches on one side and centimetres (in divisions of 5) on the other side. Write HOW HIGH? over the flower head. Punch 2 holes at top of poster, using a paper punch if you have one. Thread cord loop through holes.

Quick tip: Find other 'tall' designs in children's books. A rocket is a simple shape to draw (Fig 2).

Wood Block Puzzle

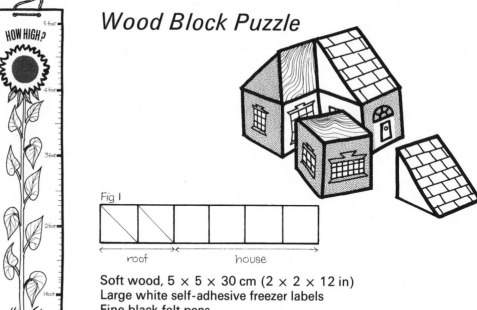

Fig 1
roof   house

Soft wood, 5 × 5 × 30 cm (2 × 2 × 12 in)
Large white self-adhesive freezer labels
Fine black felt pens
Felt pens (various colours)
Thick poster or powder paint
Varnish

Saw and sand the wood to make 6 cubes. Cut 2 of the cubes diagonally to form the 4 roof shapes (Fig 1). Paint 2 adjacent sides of each cube one colour and the other 2 sides another colour. Paint roofs a third colour. Stick windows and doors to painted sides so that a complete house can be compiled in each colour. Mark window ledges, roof tiles, etc. Varnish the blocks. Assemble the house in one colour and pack in transparent cling film wrap.

See 'Wood block village' (page 34) for window and door patterns or design your own.

Quick tip: If the blocks are very well sanded, the sawn sides can also be used to make 3 alternative house colours. Paint 2 adjacent sides in one colour, the top and side in a second colour and the bottom and side in a third colour.

Wood Block Village

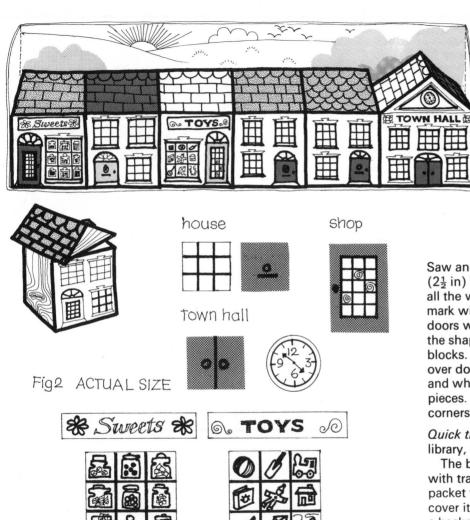

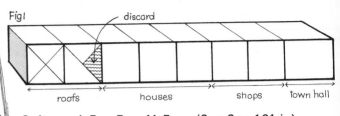

Fig 1

discard

roofs   houses   shops   town hall

Soft wood, 5 × 5 × 41·5 cm (2 × 2 × 16½ in)
Large white self-adhesive freezer labels
Fine black felt pen
Felt pens (various colours)
Thick poster or powder paint (various colours)
Varnish

house   shop

town hall

Fig 2 ACTUAL SIZE

❀ *Sweets* ❀   ◎ **TOYS** ◎

Saw and sand the wood to make 7 cubes and 1 oblong, 6·5 cm (2½ in) long. Cut 2 of the cubes into roof shapes (Fig 1). Draw all the windows and doors on labels. Use a black felt pen to mark window lines, shop names and shop contents. Colour the doors with felt pens, mark door knockers, etc. but do not outline the shapes at this stage. See Fig 2. Peel off labels and stick to blocks. Outline windows and make window ledges, windows over doors and any other details. Paint the roofs to match doors and when dry, mark tiles with black felt pen. Varnish all the pieces. Finally check that all labels are securely fixed. Glue any corners that have lifted.

Quick tips: You could create different shops and perhaps a library, church or school.

The bricks can be simply packed on a cardboard tray, covered with transparent cling wrap. The side of a medium cornflakes packet fits the village set well. Cut the box down to size and cover it with attractive paper. For added effect, line the box with a background landscape picture. Wrap the complete set with transparent cling wrap.

GIFTS

Appliqué Picture

Picture cut from printed fabric
Matching plain material, ric-rac and ribbon
Cottonwool
Cardboard
Copydex

Cut a large motif from printed fabric. Glue the upper edge to the background material. Pad the motif with cottonwool. Glue down remaining edges and stitch around entire design using small zigzag machine stitch. Some portions can be glued flat to the background, such as the stem and leaves of the flower. Glue the completed picture over the cardboard and glue ric-rac border around edge. Glue ribbon loop to back of picture.

Quick tip: Motifs cut from printed material can be stitched to children's tee shirts, kit bags, aprons, etc., omitting the stuffing.

Baby Carry-All and Changing Mat

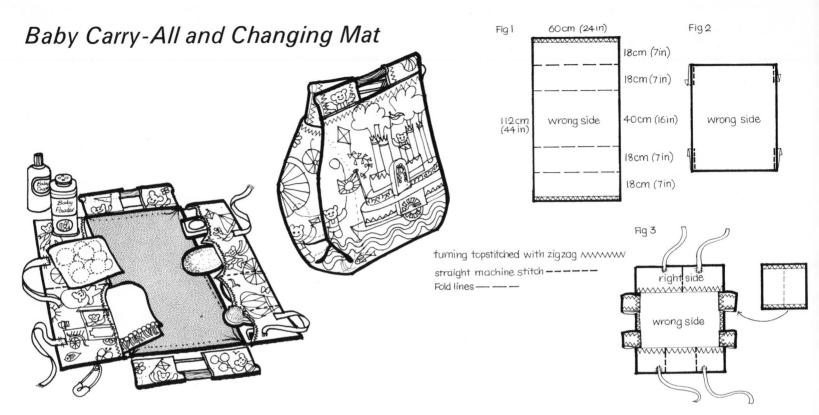

Fig 1 — 60cm (24in) — 18cm (7in) — 18cm (7in) — 112cm (44 in) — wrong side — 40cm (16in) — 18cm (7in) — 18cm (7in)

Fig 2 — wrong side

turning topstitched with zigzag ⋀⋀⋀⋀⋀⋀
straight machine stitch – – – – –
Fold lines —— — —

Fig 3 — right side — wrong side

Heavy cotton material (we used nursery curtain material), 80 cm ($\frac{7}{8}$ yd) of 122 cm (48 in) wide
Ribbon or tape, 1 metre (1 yd)
Wood dowel, 2 pieces 14 mm ($\frac{1}{2}$ in) thick, 38 cm (15 in) long
Foam rubber sheet, 36 × 54 cm (14 × 21 in)
Brightly coloured polythene, e.g. freezer batching bag, to enclose foam rubber
Transparent sticky tape
Copydex

Cut 1 piece of material 60 × 1m 15 cm (24 × 45 in) and 4 pieces 15 × 15 cm (6 × 6 in). Turnings and seams should be 14 mm ($\frac{1}{2}$ in)

throughout. We have used raw edge turnings, finished with large zigzag machine stitch. Take the large piece of material. Turn and stitch short sides (Fig 1). Turn back 18 cm (7 in) pocket at each end. Stitch seams (Fig 2). Turn pockets to right side and stitch pocket partitions (Fig 3). Press 14 mm ($\frac{1}{2}$ in) turnings along raw edges. Turn and stitch two sides of 4 small pieces of material. Fold in half and stitch in place as shown in Fig 3. Cut ribbon into 4 pieces and stitch in place (Fig 3). Make polythene envelope to contain foam rubber sheet. Seal with transparent sticky tape. Anchor to centre of carry-all with blob of copydex. Slot dowel handles in place and stitch ends of material loops.

Bath Mitt

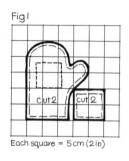

Fig 1

cut 2   cut 2

Each square = 5cm (2in)

Fig 2

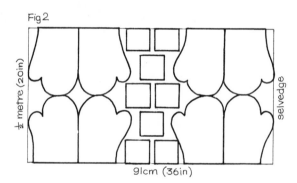

½ metre (20in)

selvedge

91cm (36in)

Towelling, ½ metre (⅝ yd) of 91 cm (36 in) wide towelling will make 4 mitts
Small soaps

Fig 1 shows mitt pattern and Fig 2 shows cutting layout.
  Hem one edge of pocket. Turn in remaining edges and stitch to mitt shape with hem facing thumb. Stitch a pocket to both back and front piece of mitt so that it can be used on either hand. Place right sides together and stitch seams. Hem cuff. Put a piece of soap in one pocket.

Beads

Fig I

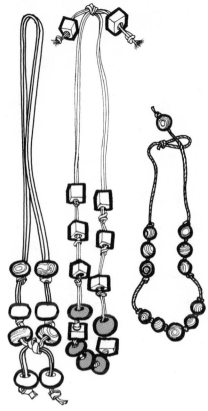

Beads (See *Quick tips*)
Leather thonging, string or cord

Make necklaces by spacing the beads with knots. The ends of the long necklaces are knotted together while the ends of the chokers are linked as shown in Fig 1.

Quick tips: We found loose beads rather expensive to buy. It is sometimes cheaper to buy threaded beads. Look out for beads and necklaces at jumble sales or make your own out of nylon reinforced clay. This does not require firing and is obtainable from toy shops.

Belts

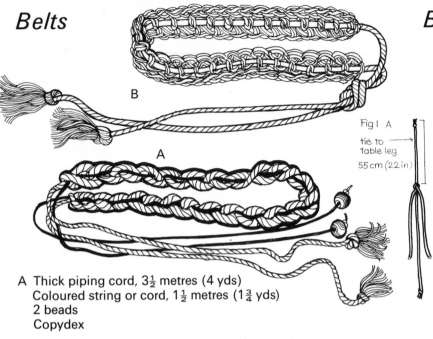

A Thick piping cord, 3½ metres (4 yds)
Coloured string or cord, 1½ metres (1¾ yds)
2 beads
Copydex

Cut a piece of piping cord, 1 m 90 cm (2¼ yards) and tie one end to a table leg. Fold the remaining piece in half and knot around long piece, securing it with copydex (Fig 1). Plait the 3 pieces together. Anchor the 2 raw ends with copydex. Using a large sewing needle, thread contrasting string or cord through plait. Add a bead to each end.

B String
Piping cord, 1½ metres (1¾ yds)
Large crochet hook

Crochet a string chain 60 cm (24 in) long. Make a row of treble crochet along chain. Work double crochet around entire piece making sure that both sides of belt are of equal tension. Use large crochet hook to thread piping cord through belt. Knot ends. Anchor cord to each end of string band with a few stitches.

Blotter

Cardboard, 1 piece 25 × 33 cm (10 × 13 in)
　　　　　　　2 pieces 4 × 25 cm (1½ × 10 in)
Material
Ribbon or braid, 15 cm (6 in)
Blotting paper

Cover the board with material on both sides, allowing enough at each end to fold over the card strips to form the pockets. Two ribbon loops are glued to one side to hold pens.

Bookmarks

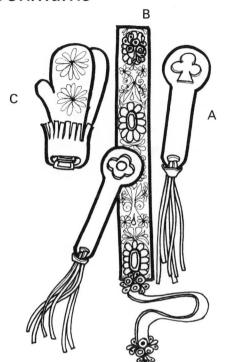

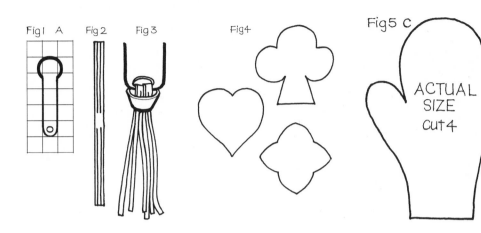

A Leather
Copydex

If both sides of leather are in good condition, simply cut out bookmark shape (Fig 1). If not, glue 2 pieces of leather, wrong sides together, before cutting out. Make a tassel from a strip of leather 1 × 20 cm ($\frac{3}{8}$ × 8 in) and cut as shown in Fig 2. Cut a hole in bookmark and thread tassel through (Fig 3). Motifs can be cut from contrasting leather and glued on (Fig 4). See 'Working with leather' (page 9).

Quick tip: ***Children** could make similar bookmarks out of felt.

B *This is suitable for **children** to make

Braid
Lace motifs
Velvet ribbon
Card
Copydex

Cover a piece of card with braid, incorporating a narrow ribbon tail at one end. Decorate with lace motifs.

C *This is suitable for **children** to make

Spring curl clip
Scraps of felt, lace, small beads etc.
Copydex

Select felt in 2 colours. Cut out 4 felt hands, 2 of each colour (Fig 5). Sandwich each side of the clip between 2 felt hands, gluing at the 'wrist'. Sew around the hands with tiny stitches. Glue a cuff of felt or lace around the 'wrist' and decorate with lace or felt flowers.

Bread Roll Cloth

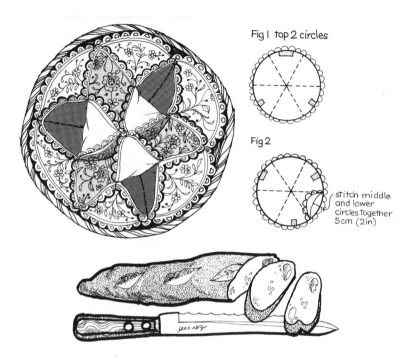

Fig 1 top 2 circles

Fig 2

stitch middle
and lower
circles together
5 cm (2 in)

Material, 3 circles of 30 cm (12 in) diameter (see *Quick tip*)
Narrow lace, 2 m 30 cm (2½ yds)
Velcro fastening, 2·5 cm (1 in)

Press a narrow turning around each circle. Stitch lace around edges, concealing turnings. Take top 2 circles. Stitch together as shown in Fig 1, adding velcro (one side of velcro is cut in half). Stitch middle and lower circles at the mid points of the 6 segments. This stitching needs to extend only 5 cm (2 in) inwards (Fig 2).

Quick tip: We have used a small print cotton fabric for the outer layers and a toning plain cotton fabric for the centre layer.

Calendars

* These can be made by **children**

Photographic mounting board (or other coloured card)
Pressed or dried flowers and leaves
Calendars
Cord
Tweezers
Uhu glue

Glue calendar and cord to a piece of card and make simple corner design with pressed or dried flowers. Use glue sparingly. Children may find pressed flowers rather delicate to handle but could put a single leaf in each corner.

Quick tips: See page 47 for another idea using dried flowers. A very simple calendar can be made by gluing a cut-out picture into the recess of a plastic carton lid and adding a hanging cord and calendar.

Candle Holders

* These can be made by **children**

Nylon reinforced clay (no firing required)
Paint (most paints will do: see clay instruction leaflet)
Taper candle

Make simple, small abstract or animal shapes with clay following the instructions on the pack and remembering that the clay will shrink slightly as it dries. Make a hole for the candle. Paint (we used metallic spray paint). The candle holders are 2·5 to 4 cm (1 to 1½ in) high.

Coathanger

Wire coathanger
Thick piping cord, 2 m 30 cm (2½ yds) (See *Quick tip*)
Small piece of tape
Copydex

Beginning at the top of the 'shoulder', bind the wire by untwisting the cord slightly and letting it recoil around the wire. Leave a 15 cm (6 in) 'tail' at each end. Bind the hook in the same way. Glue a piece of tape around the tip of the hook to secure cord. Separate a few strands of cord to bind the three ends together. Form the remainder into a plait or tassel.

Quick tip: White cotton piping cord can easily be dyed a bright colour. Form cord into a loose hank before submerging in fabric dye. Alternatively, wind a piece of brightly coloured wool around the covered wire, incorporating it into the twist of the cord.

Cotton Reel Stand

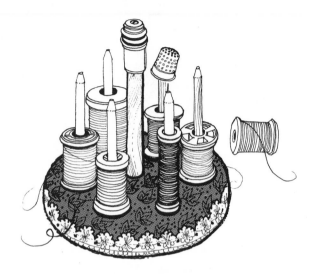

Plywood base, 14 mm ($\frac{1}{2}$ in) thick, 13 cm (5 in) diameter
Wood dowel, 1 piece 14 mm ($\frac{1}{2}$ in) thick, 13 cm (5 in) long
            6 pieces 7 mm ($\frac{1}{4}$ in) thick, 10 cm (4 in) long
Roller blind acorn
Material circle, 18 cm (7 in) diameter
Felt circle, 13 cm (5 in) diameter
Braid trim, 40 cm (16 in)
Copydex
Wood glue

Trim one end of the thicker dowel so that acorn will fit over it. Glue acorn in place and secure with screw if necessary. Sand ends of thin dowels to form points. Drill 14 mm ($\frac{1}{2}$ in) hole through centre of base. Drill 7 mm ($\frac{1}{4}$ in) holes around this. Place material over base. Mark hole positions with pencil and snip material. Push dowels into place, easing the material into the holes. Remove dowel, glue inside holes and replace dowels. Ease material round and glue to bottom of base. Cover with felt and glue braid in place.

Covered Containers

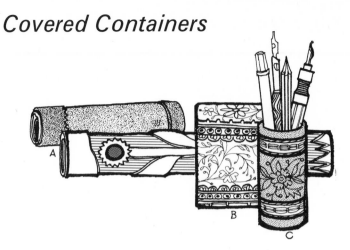

Collect sturdy boxes, tins, tubes, etc. and cover with material, felt or leather to make useful and attractive containers for jewellery, pencils, paper clips and knick-knacks. Large tins such as butchers' meat tins or large coffee tins can be made into wastepaper bins. The appeal of these items depends largely on the careful choice of fabrics and trimming materials. Small print material is particularly effective (see page 8). The possibilities are endless. Here are a few ideas.
* Some of them could be tackled by **children,** especially when felt is used.

Container
Felt, leather, material
Lace, braid, ribbon
Copydex

A Felt motifs are glued to a felt background to create flower or kite motifs. The small sweet tube is covered with two contrasting suedes.
B This is a mustard tin covered with material and trimmed with lace.
C The desk tidy is a frozen orange-juice carton covered with material and trimmed with braid.

Decorative Matchboxes and Matchbooks

D The plain bin is covered with hessian and trimmed with brown ric-rac.
   The patterned bin is covered with floral material and trimmed with ribbon and lace. If the inside of the tin is unattractive, paint it or line it with material.

E The stationery box is made from a large chocolate box. The lid is covered with a small print fabric and trimmed with lace.

* These can be made by **children**

Matchboxes (full of matches or empty for knick-knacks)
Matchbooks
Scraps of felt, leather, material, fablon, paper
Pressed flowers
Lace, braid
Copydex
Uhu glue

Here are a few examples:

A The giant-size matchbox is covered inside and out with material and trimmed with lace. The drawer handles are small curtain rings stitched in place.

B This is covered with suede and trimmed with contrasting leather cut with pinking shears. The ends of the drawer are covered and it has a leather pull-tab.
   *Children could use felt and scraps of lace or braid instead

C Glue pressed flowers to a piece of coloured paper using Uhu, and cover with clear, self-adhesive film. Glue this to matchbox or matchbook.

D Use scraps of decorative Fablon.

43

Dish Cloth Dollies

Wooden spoon or dish mop
2 all-purpose 'Jiffy' cloths
Plastic pot scourer
Soap-filled pad (wrapped in transparent
  cling wrap) or scouring cloth
2 clothes pegs
2 rubber bands
Pin
Face marked on thin card
Copydex

Wrap a folded cloth around spoon and fix with rubber band to
form skirt. Fold the second cloth to form triangular shawl. Fix
with pin. Clip peg arms to inner layers of shawl. Fix scourer to
head with elastic band. Fix card face and soap pad apron lightly
with copydex.

Quick tip: We found wide variations in the cost of the
components, so shop around.

44

Dressing Table Mirror and Comb Case

A

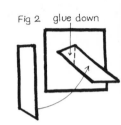

Fig I A   Fig 2   glue down

A DRESSING TABLE MIRROR

Mirror tile, 15 × 15 cm (6 × 6 in)—or mirror and contact
  adhesive
Thick card, 2 pieces each 20 × 20 cm (8 × 8 in)
          1 piece 5 × 18 cm (2 × 7 in)
Material (firm cotton with small pattern is ideal)
Lace, ½ metre (½ yard)
Copydex

Fix mirror to centre of one piece of card. Cut 13 cm (5 in) hole
in the other piece (Fig 1). Glue card to back of material, 25 ×
25 cm (10 × 10 in). Snip material from centre, almost to circle.
Cut away points and glue flaps to card, stretching material and
working in each direction alternately. Place this frame on top of
the mirror. Fold overlapping material to back and glue down,
trimming the corners. Cover back of mirror with a piece of
material. Angle the small piece of card (Fig 2), cover with
material and glue to back of mirror. Glue lace around mirror.

Quick tip: To make a wall mirror, replace card support with a
curtain ring stitched to back of mirror.

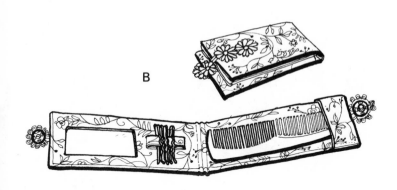

Dried Flower Hanging

Fig I

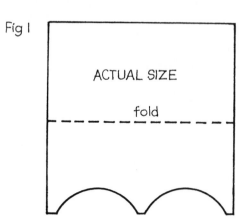

ACTUAL SIZE

fold

B COMB CASE

This is made in the same way as the dressing table mirror, using 2 pieces of card. Score a fold on both pieces before you begin. We have used a small mirror and a 13 cm (5 in) comb. A material pocket and loop have been glued in place to hold the comb and hair clips. The case is fastened by press fasteners stitched to lace daisies glued to the case. Use closely woven, firm cotton, and glue the raw edges down neatly. The overall size of this case, when open, is 7 × 27 cm (2½ × 10½ in).

Quick tip: These measurements can be adjusted to fit mirrors of different sizes. Mirrors can be cut to size and bought quite cheaply from a glass merchant.

Hessian webbing, 5 × 30 cm (2 × 12 in)
Scraps of leather
Linen carpet thread, 13 cm (5 in)
Small dried flowers
Uhu Glue

Cut out 2 pieces of leather (Fig 1).
Glue over ends of webbing.
Using a sharp needle, sew thread loop through leather on back of hanging.
Lay out dried flower design and glue in place. See *Quick tips* page 47

Quick tip: If you can find 8 cm (3 in) wide hessian webbing you can use larger dried flower heads.

Dried Flower Holders

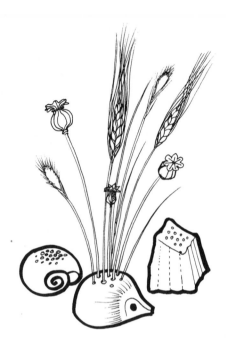

* These can be made by **children**

Nylon reinforced clay (no firing required)
Paint (most paints will do: see clay instruction leaflet)
Small dried flowers and grasses

Make simple, small abstract or animal shapes with clay, following the instructions on the pack and remembering that the clay will shrink slightly as it dries. Use a skewer and sewing needle to make holes of various sizes to take dried material. Paint (we used metallic spray paint). The dried flower holders are 2·5 to 4 cm (1 to 1½ in) high.

Dried Flower Miniatures

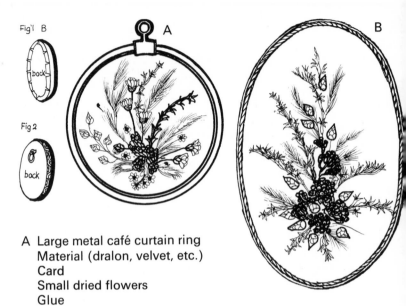

A Large metal café curtain ring
   Material (dralon, velvet, etc.)
   Card
   Small dried flowers
   Glue
   Pliers

Using pliers, gently twist small ring parallel to large ring. Glue a circle of material to a circle of card to fit ring. Glue in place. Glue flowers to background.

B Small oval basketry base
   Material
   Braid, 1 cm (⅜ in) wide
   Felt or leather
   Small dried flowers
   Small screw eye and ring
   Glue

Cover one side of base with material (Fig 1). Neaten back of base with oval of felt or leather. Glue braid around edge. Screw ring to back (Fig 2). Glue flowers to base.

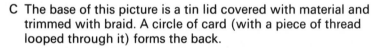

C The base of this picture is a tin lid covered with material and trimmed with braid. A circle of card (with a piece of thread looped through it) forms the back.

Quick tips: Basketry bases can be bought from handicraft shops or wooden bases can be made from 1 cm ($\frac{3}{8}$ in) plywood. Café curtain rings can be bought in shops or departments specializing in soft furnishings. Dralon sample books can often be obtained from upholsterers. Look out for any object which could be covered to form a base. Lay design on base before gluing. Use small flowers. Sea lavender is very useful for line of design and filling.

D This simple dried flower miniature is *suitable for **children** to make.

Plastic carton lid
Felt or non-fraying material
Dried flowers
Thread
Gold spray
Glue

Make a thread loop through lid. Spray rim gold. Glue circle of material into lid recess. Glue on dried flowers. For simplicity, form a star pattern, using a flower for the centre and sea lavender, grasses or pressed leaves for the points.

Quick tips: See *Quick tips* for C. Lay out design before gluing. Children may find it easier to apply glue to flowers with a matchstick or to squeeze glue very gently and carefully onto background.

Make a small mark at top of picture so that hanging thread will be in correct position when completed.

Add a calendar if you wish.

Egg Cosies

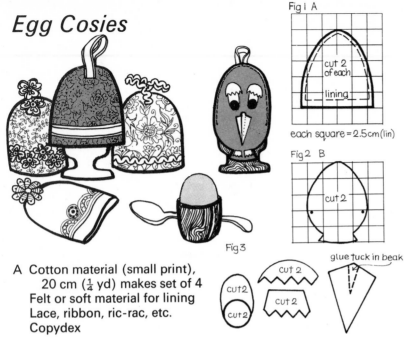

Fig I A

cut 2
of each

lining

each square = 2.5 cm (1 in)

Fig 2 B

cut 2

Fig 3

cut 2

cut 2

cut 2

cut 2

glue tuck in beak

A Cotton material (small print),
   20 cm ($\frac{1}{4}$ yd) makes set of 4
   Felt or soft material for lining
   Lace, ribbon, ric-rac, etc.
   Copydex

Cut out cosy shapes, 2 from material and 2 from lining (Fig 1). Glue lining to back of material within 7 mm ($\frac{1}{4}$ in) seam allowance. With right sides together, stitch around cosy. Turn up hem and stitch or glue over edge of lining. Turn cosy to right side. Decorate with ribbon or lace, glued or stitched in place. Make another 3 cosies to form a set.

B *This can be made by **children**

   Felt
   Heavy, non-woven interfacing for lining
   Copydex

Cut out 2 pieces of felt and 2 of interfacing (Fig 2). Glue interfacing to felt. With wrong sides together, glue or topstitch 2 sides together between dots, incorporating felt loop (8 cm (3 in) strip). Cut out felt features slightly larger than Fig 3, using pinking shears for eyebrows and feet.

Flower Press

2 pieces of plywood, 1 cm ($\frac{3}{8}$ in) thick
4 bolts, washers and wing nuts, 5 cm (2 in) long
Thick cardboard
Blotting paper
Paint or felt pens
Varnish

The plywood can be any size from 15 × 15 cm (6 × 6 in) to 30 × 30 cm (12 × 12 in). Clamp the 2 pieces together and drill a hole at each corner. Make a notch on a corresponding side of both pieces so that the holes will match when the press is reassembled. Make a flower motif on one side, using paint or felt pens. A petal potato print is simple and effective. Varnish both pieces of wood. Cut out 4 pieces of thick card and 6 pieces of blotting paper to fit the wood and cut off the corners. Compile a sandwich: one piece of card alternating with 2 pieces of paper. Assemble the flower press.

Quick tip: Sometimes stationers will sell blotting paper cheaply if you are prepared to take damaged sheets.

Gardening Apron

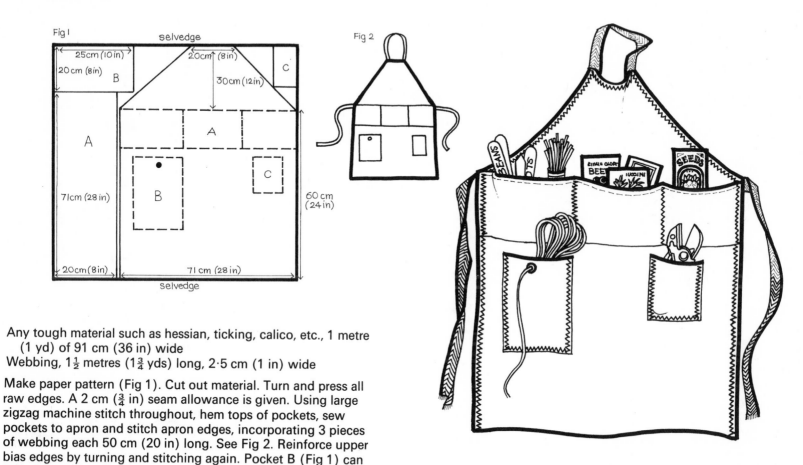

Fig 1

selvedge

25cm (10 in)
20 cm (8 in)
B

20cm (8 in)

30cm (12 in)

C

A

A

C

71cm (28 in)

B

60 cm (24 in)

20cm (8 in)

71 cm (28 in)

selvedge

Fig 2

Any tough material such as hessian, ticking, calico, etc., 1 metre (1 yd) of 91 cm (36 in) wide
Webbing, 1½ metres (1¾ yds) long, 2·5 cm (1 in) wide

Make paper pattern (Fig 1). Cut out material. Turn and press all raw edges. A 2 cm (¾ in) seam allowance is given. Using large zigzag machine stitch throughout, hem tops of pockets, sew pockets to apron and stitch apron edges, incorporating 3 pieces of webbing each 50 cm (20 in) long. See Fig 2. Reinforce upper bias edges by turning and stitching again. Pocket B (Fig 1) can include an eyelet for string.

Quick tip: Jute hessian is much less expensive than hemp hessian and can be obtained from an upholstery shop. It can be washed. If given as a personal present, the pocket can include string, tags, seeds, etc.

Hair Band

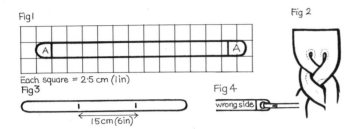

Fig 1

Each square = 2·5 cm (1in)

Fig 3

15cm (6in)

Fig 2

Fig 4

wrong side

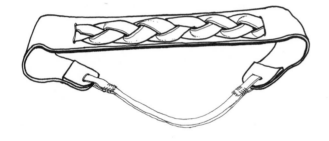

Leather
Narrow elastic, 22 cm (8½ in)
Copydex

Cut out leather hair band (Fig 1). Cut 2·5 cm (1 in) strip of
leather. Cut this into 3 lengthways, except for the last 1 cm
(½ in). Plait the 3 strands (Fig 2). Cut two 1 cm (½ in) slits in
hairband (Fig 3). Glue plait to band, threading ends through
slits and gluing on back of band. Glue 2 pieces of leather (A in
Fig 1) to each end of band to reinforce. Make small slit in each
end. Thread elastic through slits and stitch ends (Fig 4). See
'Working with leather' (page 9).

50

Hanging Wall Pockets A

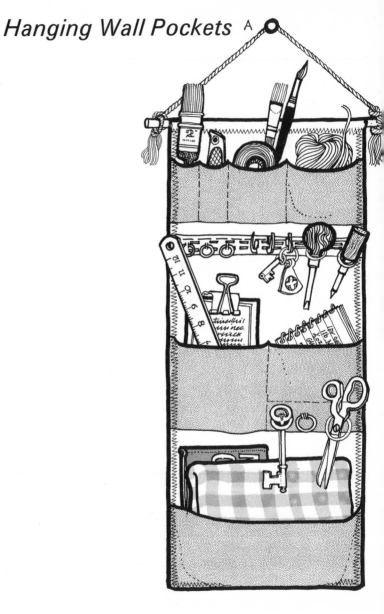

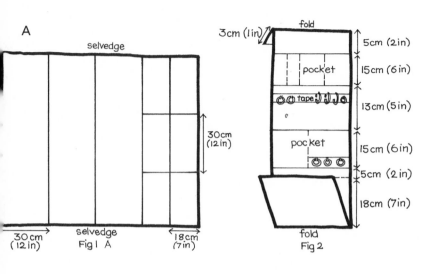

A
selvedge

30cm
(12in)

30cm
(12in) selvedge 18cm
Fig 1 A (7in)

3cm (1in)
fold

5cm (2in)
pocket
15cm (6in)
tape
13cm (5in)
pocket
15cm (6in)
5cm (2in)
18cm (7in)
fold
Fig 2

B

A Firm, plain material such as hessian
  Narrow curtain tape
  Curtain hooks and rings
  Key rings
  Piping cord, 1 metre (1 yd)
  Wood dowel or garden cane, 33 cm (13 in)

Three hanging wall pockets can be made from 1 m 30 cm
(1½ yds) of 91 cm (36 in) wide material. Fig 1 shows how to
cut these.

  To make one, cut out piece of material 91 × 30 cm (36
× 12 in) and two pockets each 18 × 30 cm (7 × 12 in). Use a
large zigzag stitch throughout. Turn and top-stitch tops of

pockets. The lower pocket is made by turning up the backing
material. Turn lower edges of pockets and top-stitch to backing.
Stitch pocket partitions. Sew on curtain tape. Turn and stitch
side seams. Turn and stitch hem for wood dowel. Add hooks,
rings and cord. See Fig 2.

B This one has a plain background and toning patchwork
  pockets, suitable for a girl's bedroom. Overall size is 46 ×
  56 cm (18 × 22 in).

Quick tips: Adjust size of hanging wall pockets to use available
material. Display a sample packed with suitable items to
demonstrate its use.

Index Recipe Book

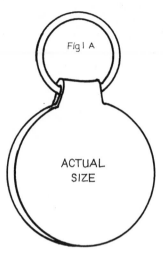

Fig l A

ACTUAL
SIZE

Key Rings

Fig 2

A Leather
   Key ring
   Copydex

Cut out simple leather tag. Thin leather should be cut double, folded over ring and glued together (Fig 1). Thick leather can be looped over as in Fig 2. Glue contrasting motif on one side. See 'Working with leather' (page 9).

B * This can be made by **children**

   Felt
   Card
   Lace
   Key ring
   Copydex

Cut out felt tag. Fold over ring. Sandwich a piece of card between layers before gluing. Add lace or felt motif. Overstitch around edge if you wish.

C * This can be made by **children**
   String
   Key ring

Fold string over ring and plait a tag. Stitch or glue ends together.

D Pressed leaf and flower
   Key ring with plastic tag
   Clear self-adhesive film
   Uhu glue

Glue pressed leaf and flower to tag. Cover with self-adhesive film.

Hard-covered notebook
Material (small print)
Adhesive index strip
Metal ruler and handicraft knife
Copydex

Cut material slightly larger than opened book. Glue the overlapping fabric inside the cover. Glue down the front and back pages to neaten. Protecting the inside of the cover with a piece of card, use ruler and knife to cut 1·5 cm ($\frac{1}{2}$ in) away from all the pages. stick index strip labels in place, adding suitable titles. Glue a piece of card marked 'Recipes' to the front of the book.

Quick tip: The front label and index strip can be left blank so that the notebook can be put to any use.

Notelets

Paper cut to 18 × 26 cm (7 × 10½ in)
Envelopes (standard letter size)
Small dried flowers and leaves
Thick marker pens—various colours
Uhu glue

Make a bold coloured border on one side of paper to tone with flowers to be used. Mark edge of envelope flap to match. Fold paper lengthways and then widthways. Lay out a simple corner design with a leaf and one or two flowers. Glue in place, using glue very sparingly. Fold a small piece of tissue paper over this corner to protect it before putting notelet in envelope.

Note Pads

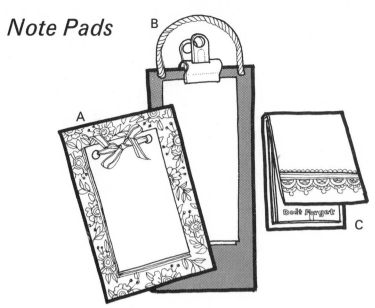

* These can be made by **children**

Cardboard
Material (small print or plain)
Bulldog clip
Ribbon, lace, cord
Paper
Copydex

A Glue a piece of material over sturdy cardboard. Glue a second piece of card over the back to cover raw edges. The paper is laced to the board with matching ribbon.
B This clipboard has been made in the same way but the paper is attached with a bulldog clip. Ordinary black clips can be painted with gloss paint. A piece of cord is knotted through holes pierced through the board.
C Divide a thick note pad into several portions. Make a simple folder of cardboard covered with material. Glue the back 2 pages of the note pad inside the back cover. Trim the front cover with lace.

Oven Mitts

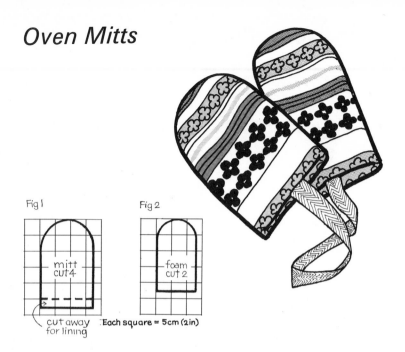

Fig 1

mitt
cut 4

cut away
for lining

Fig 2

foam
cut 2

Each square = 5cm (2in)

Heavy cotton material (furnishing fabric remnants or samples are ideal)
Lining (sheeting or curtain lining)
Sheet foam rubber, 1 cm ($\frac{3}{8}$ in) thick
Webbing, 2·5 × 38 cm (1 × 15 in)

60 cm ($\frac{5}{8}$ yd) of 122 cm (48 in) material makes 3 pairs. Cut out 4 glove pieces and 4 lining pieces (Fig 1). With right sides of gloves together sew 1·5 cm ($\frac{1}{2}$ in) seams. Likewise sew lining seams. Trim and clip curves. Cut out 2 foam pads (Fig 2). With glove inside out, place foam on palm. Slip lining, right side out, over glove. Turn up 2·5 cm (1 in) glove hem. Catch all layers of palm together in 2 or 3 places to prevent foam layer slipping. Link 2 gloves with webbing stitched to cuffs on padded sides.

Quick tip: If you wish to sell gloves individually omit webbing and stitch a tape loop to cuff.

Paper-Weight or Doorstop

Smooth pebbles
Transfers ('water-slide' rather than 'rub-down' type)
Varnish
Felt
Uhu glue

Scrub stone in soapy water. When dry apply a coat of varnish and leave to dry. Soak transfer for about 20 seconds. Remove picture carefully and dry it on a piece of paper kitchen towel. Plan the position of the picture, taking note of the shape of the stone. Put a blob of Uhu on the stone and use your finger to distribute it quickly over area to be decorated. Leave to dry for a few moments. Handling the picture very carefully, place it in position and press it very gently to smooth the surface and remove air bubbles. Varnish stone including picture. Glue a piece of felt to base.

Quick tips: Small transfers are much easier to handle. When decorating a large pebble use several small transfers rather than a large one. Alternatively, paint your own design using acrylic or oil-based paints. Model paints are useful for this.

Patchwork Cushion-Cover Kit

Patchwork Placemat

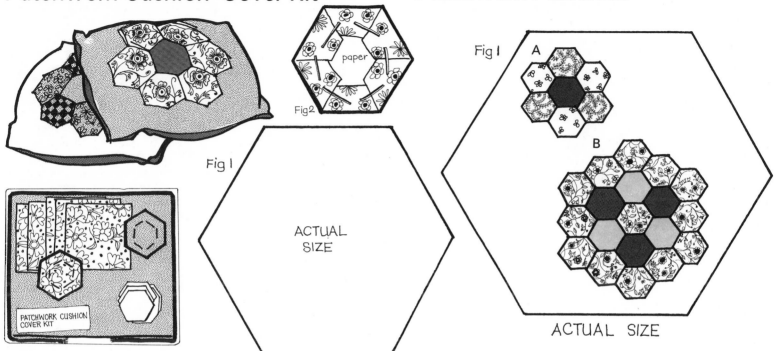

Fig 2 paper

Fig 1 ACTUAL SIZE

Fig 1 A B

ACTUAL SIZE

PATCHWORK CUSHION COVER KIT

Cushion cover material, 2 pieces 36 × 36 cm (14 × 14 in)
Patterned material, 6 pieces 10 × 10 cm (4 × 4 in)
Plain material, 1 piece 10 × 10 cm (4 × 4 in) (this can match cover material)
7 hexagons (stiff paper), see Fig 1.

Make up one of the hexagons as an example (Fig 2). Display a finished cushion on the stall and, if you like, include simple instructions in pack. Assemble the kit and pack in transparent cling film wrap or polythene bag.

Quick tip: The pack could simply contain materials for the hexagon motif which the buyer could use to decorate a table mat, child's dress, tea-cosy, etc.

Material
Felt square, 23 cm × 23 cm (9 × 9 in)
Copydex

Make up a patchwork 'flower' (A) with seven large hexagons. See template (Fig 1). Apply a few spots of copydex to the back of the flower and press the felt square in place. Carefully cut around shape. Finally, hand or machine stitch around edge of mat.

Quick tip: A 30 cm (12 in) placemat can be made by using this large hexagon, or by using the smaller hexagon on this page and adding an extra row (19 in all). See illustration B.

Patchwork Tea-Cosy

Fig1 10cm (4 in)

8cm (3 in)

1 cm (½ in)

Fig 2

A	B	A	B	A	B	A	B
C	D	C	D	C	D	C	D
E	F	E	F	E	F	E	F

side seam

Patchwork material in 6 toning designs
Lining to match
Sheet foam rubber, 28 × 44 × 1·5 cm thick (11 × 17 × ½ in)

Make a card patchwork template. The outer square gives overall size and the inner square the seam line (Fig 1). Mark squares on back of material using ballpoint pen. Cut out 24 squares (4 in each colour).

If you are inexperienced in patchwork design, follow the pattern in Fig 2, balancing light and dark tones. Lay your squares out before sewing. Then stitch them together into 3 strips of 8. Press seams, then stitch strips together lengthways, matching corners. Fold material with right sides together and stitch side and top seams. Make lining the same size. With cosy inside out and lining right side out, fit foam and lining over patchwork. Tack 3 layers together across top of cosy. Turn in patchwork and lining seam allowances at lower edges and neatly over-stitch.

Quick tip: You can use 12 different toning fabrics, making the back different from the front.

Pincushions

Fig1 A

Fig 3 C

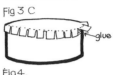

glue

Fig 4

A

C

B

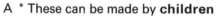

A * These can be made by **children**

6 squares of felt, 8 × 8 cm (3 × 3 in)
Stuffing (2 pairs of nylon tights, chopped up, will do)

Topstitch the felt squares together (Fig 1) to form a cube. Stuff before sewing final edge.

Quick tip: Glue felt 'dots' to sides of cube if you wish it to represent a dice.

B *These can be made by **children**

2 large hexagons of felt or fabric (Fig 2)
Lace
Stuffing

Pin and topstitch the hexagons together, sandwiching the lace between the 2 layers. Stuff the cushion before sewing the final side. Glue or stitch a lace motif to the centre. If using material, press in 7 mm (¼ in) turnings before you begin.

ACTUAL SIZE

Fig 2 B

Serviettes and Rings

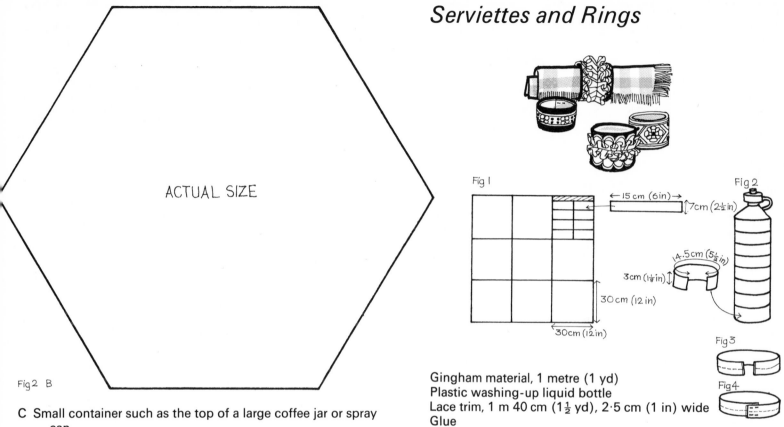

Fig 1

← 15 cm (6 in) →

7 cm (2½ in)

Fig 2

4.5 cm (5½ in)

3 cm (1⅛ in)

30 cm (12 in)

30cm (12 in)

Fig 3

Fig 4

C Small container such as the top of a large coffee jar or spray
   can
   Small pieces of material, felt, braid, lace
   Stuffing, including a layer of foam sheet or wadding
   Glue

Fill container with stuffing topped with a circle of foam sheet.
Cut out a circle of material about 2·5 cm (1 in) larger than
container. Lay this over the stuffing and glue around rim (Fig 3).
Cut away any excess material. Glue a strip of material, felt or
braid around the container (Fig 4) and trim with lace or velvet
ribbon.

Gingham material, 1 metre (1 yd)
Plastic washing-up liquid bottle
Lace trim, 1 m 40 cm (1½ yd), 2·5 cm (1 in) wide
Glue
Stapler

These materials make 8 sets. Cut out gingham material (Fig 1).
Cut rings from plastic bottle and cut to size (Fig 2). Glue
material to plastic so that seam is on outside and ends overlap
plastic slightly. Glue ends to neaten (Fig 3). Form into ring and
staple. Glue lace around ring. Fray edges of serviette square.
Roll up serviette and place in ring. Sell as pairs or whole sets.

Quick tip: Make a variety of serviette rings using odd scraps of
material, braid and lace.

Shopping Bags

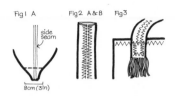

Hessian (inexpensive jute hessian,
    obtainable from upholsterers is ideal)
Dark brown thread
Felt and copydex or permanent marker pens

A   LARGE BAG

2 main pieces, 40 × 40 cm (16 × 16 in)
1 pocket, 25 × 25 cm (10 × 10 in)
2 handles, 5 × 46 cm (2 × 18 in)

$1\frac{1}{2}$ metres ($1\frac{5}{8}$ yd) makes 3 bags. Allow 1·5 cm ($\frac{1}{2}$ in) for
hems and seams. Turn in seam allowance of pocket. Use large
zigzag machine stitch to hem top of pocket and to sew to front.
With right sides together sew front to back. With bag wrong
side out, match bottom and side seams and stitch across corners
(Fig 1). Hem top of bag. Make handles (Fig 2). Stitch securely
to bag and fray ends (Fig 3). Glue a felt motif to pocket or make
a design with marking pens.

B   CHILD'S BAG

2 main pieces, 25 × 25 cm (10 × 10 in)
1 pocket, 15 × 15 cm (6 × 6 in)
2 handles, 5 × 46 cm (2 × 18 in)

70 cm ($\frac{3}{4}$ yd) makes 3 bags. This bag is made in the same way
as the large bag except that the corners are not inserted. (Not
illustrated.)

Quick tips: Hessian webbing of suitable width could be used for
handles.
    Make simple shopping bags from any tough fabric.

Shoulder Bag

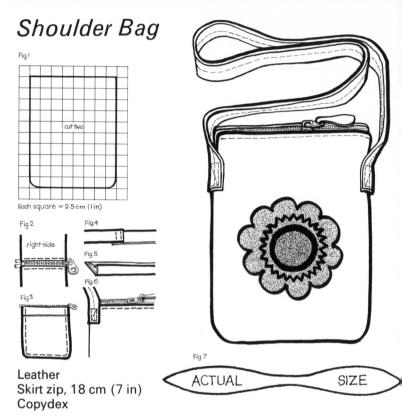

Leather
Skirt zip, 18 cm (7 in)
Copydex

Cut out bag (Fig 1). Make 2·5 cm (1 in) turning towards wrong
side at top edge of each piece. Glue down. Topstitch zip to
these edges (Fig 2). Open zip. With right sides together, sew
seams (Fig 3). Cut out two strips of leather, 5 × 46 cm (2 ×
18 in). Glue and stitch ends together (Fig 4). Fold and glue
lengthways (Fig 5). Topstitch down centre of handle. Topstitch
to sides of bag (Fig 6). Trace Fig 7 to make a leather tag. Thread
through hole in zip—pull and glue 2 sides together (Fig 7).
Using reverse side of leather, cut out motif and glue to bag.

Quick tips: Zips can be obtained from jumble sale garments. See
'Working with leather' (page 9).

Stationery Holder

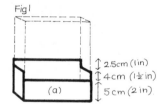

Fig1

(a)

2·5cm (1in)
4cm (1½ in)
5cm (2 in)

Cardboard box (e.g. small breakfast cereal box)
Material (small print)
Lace
Copydex
Paper, envelopes

Choose a box of suitable size to match the notepaper. Cut the box down as shown in Fig 1. Cut a piece of card the same size as (a) to form the divider. Cover the entire box with material. Cover the divider with material leaving an overlapping flap along one edge with which to glue it to the base of the box. Leave the sides free so that its position can be adjusted. All seams can be glued down. Glue lace trim in place.

String and Tape Stand

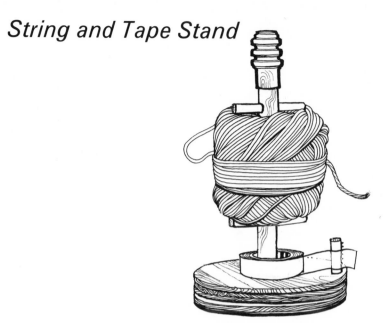

Plywood base, 14 mm (½ in) thick, 13 cm (5 in) diameter
Wood dowel, 1 piece 14 mm (½ in) thick, 15 cm (6 in) long
2 pieces 7 mm (¼ in) thick, 6 cm (2½ in) long
1 piece 7 mm (¼ in) thick, 4 cm (1½ in) long
Roller blind acorn
Hacksaw blade, 2·5 cm (1 in)
Wood glue
Varnish

Drill two 7 mm (¼ in) holes through the largest dowel, allowing enough space for a ball of string between them, and a roll of tape below. Slot 7 mm (¼ in) dowels through holes but do not glue. Trim top of 14 mm (½ in) thick dowel so that acorn will fit. Glue acorn onto dowel and secure with screw if necessary. Glue dowel into 14 mm (½ in) hole drilled into centre of base. Slot hacksaw blade into remaining dowel and glue this into a 7 mm (¼ in) hole drilled near edge of base. Varnish the stand.

Quick tip: The holder can be free-standing or screwed to a wall.

Tea-Pot Stand

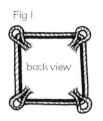

Fig I.

back view

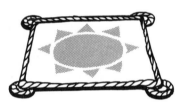

Tool Roll

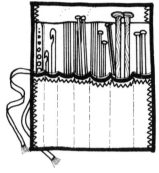

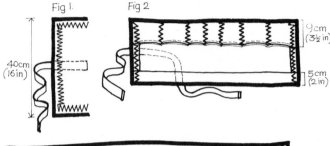

Fig I.
40cm (16in)

Fig 2
9cm (3½ in)
5cm (2 in)

Ceramic tile, 11 cm (4¼ in) square
Twisted cord, 71 cm (28 in) long, 3 mm (⅛ in) thick
Felt, 12 cm (4½ in) square
Uhu glue

Glue 51 cm (20 in) of cord around edge of tile, twisting the ends together. Cut remainder of cord into 5 cm (2 in) lengths. Glue to corners on back of tile (Fig 1), Glue felt to back of tile, covering cord ends.

Tough material, 45 × 50 cm (18 × 20 in)
Webbing, 2·5 × 75 cm (1 × 30 in)

This is suitable for small carpentry tools. Use contrasting thread and a large zigzag stitch throughout. Turn and stitch a narrow hem around material, incorporating webbing (Fig 1). Fold longest sides and stitch partitions, 2·5 to 8 cm (1 to 3 in) apart (Fig 2).

Quick tip: The tool roll can be adapted to accommodate knitting needles.

Triangular Headscarf

Fig I

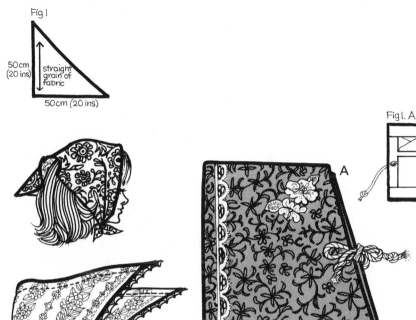

50cm (20 ins) — straight grain of fabric
50cm (20 ins)

Lightweight material such as cotton lawn, 50 × 50 cm (20 × 20 in) makes 2 scarves
Narrow lace, 1 metre (40 in) (optional)

Cut out triangle of material (Fig 1). Press corners to wrong side. Press narrow turning around all sides. Turn and press again. Stitch turnings. Stitch lace on wrong side if required.

Writing Folders

Cardboard
Material (small print)
Lace, cord, ribbon, eyelets
Press fastener
Copydex
Paper, envelopes, blotting paper

Fig I. A

B

Basically these are folders made out of cardboard, 28 × 40 cm (11 × 16 in), covered with material. Fold raw edges under and glue with copydex. Thick cardboard needs to be scored down the fold. Sizes can be adjusted to match materials and paper available.

A The material is folded up at the top and bottom to form pockets on the inside to hold blotter, paper and envelopes (Fig 1). Cord ties are knotted through holes made with eyelets. The front has been trimmed with lace and a lace flower motif.

B The stamp pocket, blotter corners and stationery pocket are pieces of card covered with material and glued to the folder A material strap supports the folder when open. The pockets have been trimmed with motifs cut from a lace strip. The folder is fastened by press fasteners stitched to lace daisies glued to the folder.

61

CHRISTMAS

Christmas Stockings

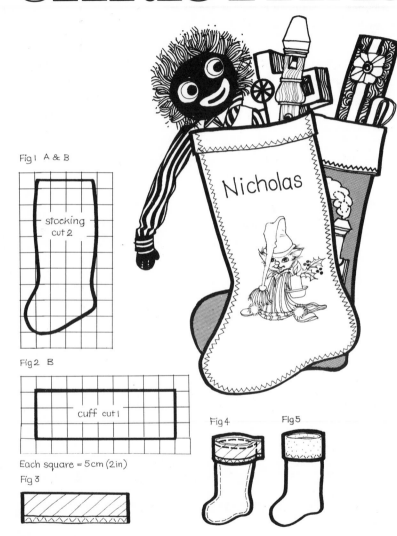

Fig 1 A & B

stocking cut 2

Fig 2 B

cuff cut 1

Each square = 5 cm (2 in)

Fig 3

Fig 4   Fig 5

A QUICK AND EASY STOCKING

Heavy non-woven interfacing, 1 metre ($1\frac{1}{8}$ yd) of 91 cm (36 in)
   wide makes 4 stockings
Red thread
Red tape
Red thick marking pen
Picture cut from used Christmas card
Copydex

Cut out stocking shapes. See pattern Fig 1. Use large zigzag
machine stitch throughout. Turn and topstitch tops of stocking
pieces. Glue wrong side of remaining edges and stick 2 stocking
pieces together. Topstitch around stocking, reinforcing the
stitching at the opening edge. There is no need for a turned
seam as this material does not fray. Stitch a tape loop to the top.
Glue picture to stocking. Make faint pencil guidelines and print
child's name across top of stocking. This can be added as the
stockings are sold.

B VELVET CUFFED STOCKINGS

Material (See *Quick tip*)
Velvet, corduroy, needlecord, satin, etc. for cuffs
Picture cut from used Christmas card
Copydex

Cut out stocking shapes (Fig 1) and cuff (Fig 2). With right
sides together, sew stocking pieces together with 1·5 cm ($\frac{1}{2}$ in)
seams. Turn and topstitch top of cuff (Fig 3). With right side of
cuff facing wrong side of stocking, stitch upper edges together.
Then stitch cuff side seam (Fig 4). Turn stocking to right side.
Fold over cuff (Fig 5) and glue picture to stocking.

Quick tip: Use any plain bright material. Old cotton sheets can
be dyed. A large tin of dylon will dye $2\frac{1}{2}$ lb of cloth. Discard any
very worn patches.

Christmas Tree Angels

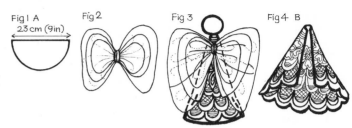

A Ping-pong ball
   Stiff paper
   Gold spray paint
   Gold doily, 23 cm (9 in) diameter (or spray a white doily)
   Nylon net
   Black marking pen
   Stapler
   Uhu glue

Cut a semi-circle from paper (Fig 1). Form and staple into cone. Trim base. Glue $\frac{1}{2}$ doily around cone. Using sharp, pointed scissors, cut a 14 mm ($\frac{1}{2}$ in) hole in ping-pong ball. Wedge onto a roll of newspaper and spray gold. Glue ball onto cone and mark face and hair. Spray net lightly. Cut out 3 rectangles, 13 cm (5 in) deep and 15 cm (6 in), 18 cm (7 in) and 20 cm (8 in) wide respectively. Trim the corners and place on top of one another. Gather the centre with thread (Fig 2). Glue to cone and anchor wing tips with staples (Fig 3). Cut out 3 net circles between 2·5 cm (1 in) and 5 cm (2 in) diameter and glue the 3 layers to head.

B * This can be made by **children**

This is a simpler version. Instead of using net fabric for wings and halo, use a gold doily. Make the cone and head as in A but use just $\frac{1}{3}$ of the doily to cover the cone, leaving a gap at the back if necessary. Use the remainder of the doily to form wings (Fig 4). Glue this to the back of the angel. The halo is a motif cut from a doily.

Quick tip: The angels can be silver instead of gold and can be quite effective even without the use of metallic spray paint.

Flower and Candle Arrangements

A Plastic washing-up liquid bottle
   Florists' ribbon, 5 cm (2 in) wide × 1 metre (1 yd)
      (sufficient for 2 containers)
   Copydex
   Stapler
   Oasis
   Flowers and greenery

Cut the bottle down to a depth of 5 cm (2 in) leaving a 2·5 cm
(1 in) wide handle at each side (Fig 1). Staple handles together
(Fig 2). Strip some of the ribbon in half and glue to handle.
Glue ribbon around base to cover plastic. Wedge a piece of
Oasis in container so that it protrudes above the rim and make a
simple floral arrangement.

B Oasis dish or suitable plastic carton
   Oasis
   Real flowers, crêpe flowers or tissue paper flowers (see page
      66)
   Greenery
   Candle

Wedge a piece of Oasis in the dish and make a simple
arrangement around a candle. If it is to be sold at a Christmas
Bazaar, use evergreen leaves and paper flowers in well soaked
Oasis. This will last for several weeks. Take care to keep paper
flowers dry.

C Polystyrene ceiling tile
   Oasis and Oasis pin holder
   Tinfoil
   Evergreen leaves
   Ribbon bows (see page 67)
   Candle

Cut a star shape from the tile using sharp scissors (Fig 3). Soak
a block of Oasis thoroughly in water and wrap in foil. Pierce star
with pin holder and anchor Oasis on the pins. Arrange leaves
and bows around the candle.

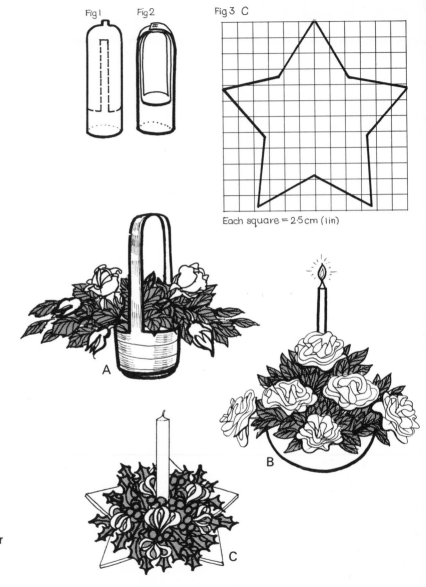

Fig 1   Fig 2   Fig 3 C

Each square = 2·5 cm (1 in)

A

B

C

Gift Boxes

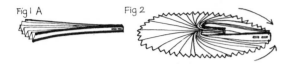

A Box
   Plain wrapping paper (gold, silver or bright colour)
   Gold or Silver doilies
   Crêpe paper
   Copydex

Cover box lid with paper, gluing edges inside sides of lid. Use a doily and a crêpe paper rosette to decorate top of lid. The edge can be trimmed with the border of a doily.

   Crêpe paper rosette: Cut a piece of crêpe paper using pinking shears, 5 × 60 cm (2 × 24 in). Fold into a concertina widthways and glue or staple at one end (Fig 1). Fan the folds out, and staple the 2 edges together (Fig 2). Glue circle of paper or doily motif to centre. Adjust folds when gluing to box lid.

Quick tip: Make matching gift tags (See B on page 66).

B The lid is covered with gift wrapping paper and decorated with a ribbon bow.

C Christmas tree decorations
   Small boxes
   Coloured foil paper
   Gift ribbon
   Copydex

Cover boxes with foil paper. Add ribbon, including loop to hang. Cut out contrasting foil stars (or use doily motifs).

Gift Tags

* These can all be made by **children**

A Coloured card or cartridge paper
   Pressed flowers and leaves
   Embroidery threads
   Felt pen
   Tweezers
   Uhu glue

Cut out folded cards or tags of different shapes. Pinking shears give a decorative edge. Punch a hole or make a slot and loop a piece of thread through. A border can be marked with felt pen. Glue pressed material to card. A single leaf or flower is adequate.

Quick tip: Folded gift cards can be sold with small envelopes.

B Coloured card
   Gold or silver doily
   Black felt pen
   Gift ribbon
   Pinking shears
   Copydex

Cut small motifs from doily and glue to card shape, cut with pinking shears if you have them. Loop a narrow piece of ribbon through a slit in the card.

Quick tip: Save the brightly coloured card usually found in a packet of doilies.

Small Artificial Flowers and Bows

A CRÊPE PAPER FLOWER

Crêpe paper
Fuse wire or thin florists' wire
Florists' tape (optional)

Fold crêpe paper to cut out many petals at a time. Each flower needs 9 petals (Fig 1). Curve tips of petals by stroking backwards between thumb and closed scissors. With curve facing backwards shape the petal by stretching the lower part between thumbs and index fingers to make indentation (Fig 2). Wind wire around 1st petal (Fig 3) and wire on each petal in turn. Bind wire with green tape.

B TISSUE PAPER FLOWER

Tissue paper
Fuse wire or florists' wire
Florists' tape (optional)
Blu-tack

Cut many layers of tissue paper at a time—10 petals for each flower (Fig 4). Pierce petals with wire and fix at front and back with blu-tack. Place thumb and index finger into flower to spread petals and crimp them in different directions.

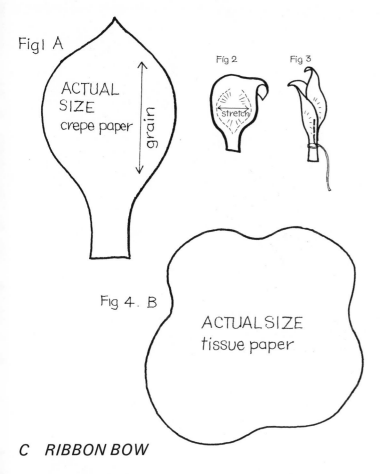

Fig1 A

ACTUAL
SIZE
crepe paper

grain

Fig 2

stretch

Fig 3

Fig 4. B

ACTUAL SIZE
tissue paper

C RIBBON BOW

Narrow gift ribbon or florists' ribbon, 46 cm (18 in)
Florists' tape (optional)

Fold ribbon to make 3 loops. Wind wire around base, twisting
the loops in different directions. Cover wire if you like. Take care
not to wet gift ribbon.

Quick tip: See flower arrangements on page 64.

PLANTS, PRODUCE AND FOOD

A plant stall needs to be carefully organized before the doors are opened to ensure that all the goods are clearly named and priced by someone who knows the difference between an antirrhinum and an aster! Stack pots in seed trays or in large, shallow cardboard boxes obtained from your grocer. Prop the boxes up so that they are tilted forwards. Standardize prices as much as possible and confine all identically priced plants to the same part of the stall. It is a great help to list the plants and prices on a blackboard or cardboard poster at eye level. Delete any plants which are sold out as the sale progresses. Wear an apron with a large pocket in which to keep your change as this is much more convenient than a money box on the stall.

Plastic yoghurt or margarine cartons are ideal for most small plants as it is not worth spending much on the containers if the contents are to be planted out. Plant pots can be used for houseplants and it may be worth investing in some peat pots for individual plants which you know will fetch a good price, such as the more exotic herbs, courgettes, peppers, tomatoes, etc. Look out for economy packs of peat pots at your local nursery. Plan ahead and save any suitable plastic or polystyrene containers.

Tie into bunches and store in buckets of water together with a price card slotted into a bamboo stick.

DRIED FLOWERS AND HERBS

Hang bunches of dried flowers, grasses, glycerined beech leaves, honesty and lavender on a 'clothes-line' over the stall. Make up cellophane packs of dried flowers, lavender, herbs and pot-pourri. Alternatively you can use scraps of fine fabric, organdie, muslin, lace, etc. to make lavender bags, pot-pourri sachets and herb pillows.

FRESH HERBS

All herb plants sell well. Those best grown from seed such as parsley, chervil, borage and basil can be sown in compost in plastic cartons or peat pots. Tough roots such as mint, sorrel and thyme can be wrapped in moist newspaper and secured with a rubber band or string. Tuck a cardboard name label under the band and keep paper damp. They can be prepared a day or two in advance. A clump of chives can be divided and planted in plastic cartons or wrapped in damp newspaper. Cuttings of rosemary, sage and bay can be similarly planted or packed. Pack sprigs of fresh herbs on a polystyrene meat tray covered with transparent cling wrap.

PLANT CUTTINGS

Many popular indoor plants such as spider plants, Busy Lizzie and ivy are very easy to propagate and can be sold in individual plant pots.

Plant rooted shrub cuttings in individual pots, clearly named and priced.

Divide hardy herbaceous plants and wrap roots in damp newspaper, tied and labelled (see Herbs).

BULBS

Spring bulbs are popular at Autumn bazaars. Buy bulbs and bulb fibre in bulk to cut the cost. A local nursery may be able to help. *Children can plant several crocus bulbs in a ½ lb decorative margarine carton.

FRESH FRUIT AND VEGETABLES

Pack surplus home-grown apples, pears, plums, tomatoes, runner beans, etc. on polystyrene trays covered with cling wrap, or in paper or polythene bags. Try to standardize pack weights and prices. Your local greengrocer may lend you some wooden stacking fruit trays to store soft fruit. String up onions and garlics to fetch a better price. Make an attractive display with these and other vegetables such as marrows, cabbages, bunches of carrots and radishes, etc., depending on the season. A school may be able to sell produce grown in its own garden or greenhouse. Later in the Autumn you may be able to acquire surplus walnuts, sweet chestnuts, hazelnuts and almonds.

VEGETABLE PLANTS

Plant very small seedlings of lettuces and the brassicas ($\frac{1}{2}$ dozens) in plastic cartons. Label them clearly, as brussels sprouts look much like winter cabbage to the inexperienced eye. Larger plants can be packed in damp newspaper (see Herbs). Sell marrows, courgettes and tomatoes in individual plastic cartons. Good-sized, staked tomato plants can be sold individually in large (4 litre) plastic ice cream cartons. Early lettuces and spring cabbages can be sold at Autumn bazaars.

*Children enjoy sowing mustard and cress seeds on a pad of wet absorbent paper in a polystyrene meat tray, following the instructions on the seed packet.

CHRISTMAS DECORATIONS

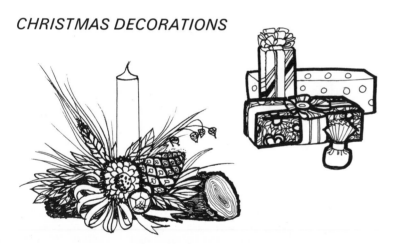

Christmas decorations such as holly wreaths, logs and table arrangements are always popular. Plane off one side of smaller logs to make them stable. Saw large logs in half lengthways and drill a hole for a candle. Decorate one with dried or artificial material to demonstrate their possibilities. Logs can also be sold as firewood.

Page 64 gives ideas for simple floral arrangements.

70

FOOD

Cakes are popular and profitable at any time of the year. Make sure you have a good supply of paper plates, paper bags, transparent cling wrap and some cake boxes. Many bakers' shops will sell these for a few pence. Pack and label all large cakes before the sale starts. Individual cakes can be laid out on trays, grouped according to price.

Pack sweets, biscuits, truffles, shortbread, etc. in pretty boxes, jars or tins, lined with paper doilies and trimmed with ribbon. Start collecting suitable containers well in advance. Jars of pickles, chutneys, jams and marmalade can be brightened up with attractive labels (bought or home-made) and pretty pot covers. Use pinking shears to cut out a circle of cotton material (gingham or small flower print for example). Fit this over the jar and anchor with an elastic band. If the jar has a screw top, use copydex to glue the material to the rim of the top. To make a more elaborate cover, gather the circle of material with shirring elastic and trim with lace.

Cold fruit drinks are welcomed by shoppers during the summer months. Fresh herbs and fruits make attractive garnishes. Float a sprig of mint, lemon balm, lemon thyme or a bright starry borage flower on the drink or use strawberries, cherries or slices of citrus fruits cut into attractive shapes.